# ISRAEL
## The Way It Was

*Haim Gershoni*

A Herzl Press Publication
Cornwall Books
NEW YORK ● LONDON ● TORONTO

© 1989 by Rosemont Publishing and Printing Corporation

Cornwall Books
440 Forsgate Drive
Cranbury, NY 08512

Cornwall Books
25 Sicilian Avenue
London WC1A 2QH, England

Cornwall Books
P.O. Box 488, Port Credit
Mississauga, Ontario
Canada L5G 4M2

Herzl Press
515 Park Avenue
New York, NY 10022

The paper used in this publication meets the requirements
of the American National Standard for Permanence of Paper
for Printed Library Materials Z39.48-1984.

**Library of Congress Cataloging-in-Publication Data**

Gershoni, Haim.
  Israel : the way it was / Haim Gershoni.
  p cm
  "A Herzl Press publication."
  ISBN 0-8453-4822-1 (alk. paper)
  1. Gershoni, Haim.  2. Jews, American—Israel—Biography.
  3. Israel-Arab War, 1948–1949—Naval operations.  4. Immigrants-
  -Israel—Biography.  I. Title.
  DS113.8.A4G47   1989
  956.94'05'0924—dc19
  [B]                                                      88-47908
                                                              CIP

PRINTED IN THE UNITED STATES OF AMERICA

*To Yona*

# Contents

# Preface

The events surrounding Israel's birth and early years were filled with a wonder and excitement that has largely been forgotten. The magic has been replaced with dates and events that are almost impossible for today's generation to appreciate.

This is a personal account of those times told by one who was a part of those events. It is hoped that the anecdotes of both minor and major events will help today's reader to not only know more about what really happened, but to understand the feelings and attitudes of the people involved.

If you care to join me, I would like to take you back to 1948 and show you "the way it was."

# ISRAEL
## The Way It Was

# 1
# What's It All About?

We used to say, "If you don't believe in miracles, you're not a realist." Actually, we saw a lot of truth in this, for in 1948 each day seemed to offer new evidence of the supernatural. Unfortunately, we got to the point where we often counted on such miracles to solve our problems.

It's a pity that these magic times are slipping into the distant past recalled to us mainly by historians citing facts and figures, but largely ignoring the many human touches that make the past come to life. In a sense, trying to relate to the past by analyzing only historical data is much like kissing a photograph. Personal contact certainly makes a difference.

For this reason, I'd like to take you back to those days and share with you my personal experiences so that perhaps you too can feel how it really was. To be sure, I can't tell you about everything that happened, because I only saw a part of the picture. However, by one of those quirks of fate, I was in the right place at the right time. This is essentially an account of the events that I saw during those early days of Israel's history.

Since this is a personal account, let me start with just a few words about your guide and the world as we saw it in the days preceeding Israel's independence.

I was born in Chicago of parents also born in the same city. We lived in a very comfortable suburb as a typical American family. Well, almost typical—we were Jews. Now, there are all kinds of Jews, but we were the kind who never had a Christmas tree, yet ate bacon with our waffles on Sunday morning.

There were only a few Jewish families in Winnetka, Illinois, in those days, so I grew up with Christian friends. We played football in the park and basketball at the community center. We lived on our bicycles, and at sixteen everyone learned to drive. Each Sunday my buddies were bundled off to Sunday schools at their local churches while my brother, sister, and I took the train to Glencoe where we went to religious school at the North Shore Congregation of Israel—a very reformed temple.

There, we developed a superficial acquaintance with Moses and a few of our other forefathers. We were also introduced to the facts of life, such as anti-Semitism. We didn't actually meet this phenomenon in our sheltered community, but later, events more or less did live up to our expectations.

Midwest America before television and transatlantic flying was very far from the current events of Europe. We occasionally read about Hitler and his rise to power, but this was all too far away to be real. Our lives and thoughts were centered on American issues.

We were products of the Great Depression in the United States and a college education was considered essential for future success, so in 1939 I started my studies of naval architecture and marine engineering at MIT. Then, in the middle of my junior year, we were at war. Within weeks most of my class of naval architects volunteered for the navy. Our studies were accelerated, and we finished a year later with both a degree and a commission in the navy.

During the next three years I was a ship repair officer, and while we followed every twist and turn of each battle, the fate of Europe's Jews more or less remained in the background. One must realize that this period was unlike any before or after World War II, for everyone was totally involved in the war effort to the point that it became a way of life to which we saw no end. We had no way of knowing that atom bombs would one day end the war overnight.

Then, literally, one day it was over, and we began to consider something that had never entered our minds—life as civilians.

The country was in an upheaval, and we really could not know what we wanted, so my wife Marilyn (of but a few months) and I decided to go back to school. We moved to Cambridge, Massachuttes, where we spent a lovely year unwinding. I obtained my M.S. at MIT, and Marilyn studied painting.

At the end of the year the Gershenow minifamily, which now included a yet unborn son, David, moved to Great Neck, New York. There I became manager of Halmor Knitting Mills—a family enterprise. A civilian at last, with time to live a normal life and think about the world around us. To most Americans, the war was over and they began to lead normal lives. However, as Hitler's final solution was revealed, we Jews went from the horror of World War II to that of the Holocaust. Despite the fact that Marilyn and I were both second-generation Americans, we could not divorce ourselves from the fate of Europe's Jews. We felt that we must do something to help, but we really had no idea of how to go about it.

This story really begins one evening when Norm Weisman, a close friend, mentioned that he had been to a most interesting luncheon. It seemed that a group of Jews, mainly New Yorkers, identified with the displaced persons in Europe sufficiently to want to do something to help.

It was clear by then that the only place the refugees in Europe could go was Palestine, but at that time the British were still in control and refused to allow any such immigration. The Jewish community of Palestine, however, was already active in smuggling Jews out of Europe in broken-down ships to Palestine. This was strictly a pauper's effort badly in need of financial help, and New York was of course the place to raise the necessary funds.

Each week this group, under the leadership of Rudolf Sonneborn, had a fund-raising luncheon at the McAlpin Hotel in New York. Simple plates of sandwiches and pots of coffee, were followed by speakers fresh from Palestine to tell us was was really happening. It was there that the newspaper accounts came to life. People did donate money on the spot, but essentially, the main effort was to organize parlor meetings in private homes. Speakers from Palestine would attend these meetings and this was where the serious fund-raising took place.

Norm and I were definitely of the young generation not old enough to have the clout for fund-raising, but we did flit about the fringes, as moths about a flame, and undertook all sorts of odd jobs.

"Do you know anyone who is a radio ham and has a large transmitter at home?" One of the easy ones, for Marvin Chaikin, an ex-navy communications officer, was just the man, and he lived in the same building as I.

"Where can we get an aerial camera?" Another easy errand. One of our fathers' friends was in the camera business, and was pleased to donate one.

During the following months these Thursday luncheons became almost a way of life. In terms of today's society it might seem like a dilettante's pastime, but in terms of our very young lives, this was one of the only things that made us feel as if we were doing something to help.

Unfortunately, even this small gesture came to an end, for during the winter of 1947–48, it became impossible to obtain enough rayon yarn to operate our knitting mill. It was decided to close the mill for a period and I, together with my family, went to Chicago to work with my uncle Frank in another part of the family business.

When asked what he did for a living, my father would often reply that he was in ladies' dresses. Well, for the next several months I was in ladies' underpants.

I missed the Thursday briefings at the McAlpin, but the newspapers

kept us pretty well informed. We read all about the U.N. Subcommittee on Palestine, and when the majority report of 26 September 1947
called for the partition of Palestine into Jewish and Arab states, we
suddenly felt that maybe there really would be a Jewish homeland in
our time.

Then, on the twenty-ninth of November, the United Nations voted
to accept the subcommittee's recommendations and we were over-
joyed. Looking back on this it is hard to appreciate our elation, since
today we are quite blasé about the existence of the State of Israel.
Moreover, decisions of the United Nations are no longer respected as
in those days.

One ominous cloud that slipped by without our realizing its por-
tent, was the announcement by the British government in December,
that they would not implement this U.N. decision. In essence, the
British simply made it clear that they were leaving Palestine.

It was not until later that we found this policy to be the beginning of
a devastating series of acts aimed at preventing the survival of the
coming Jewish State. However, in our elation, the only thing that
mattered was the fact that there was to be a Jewish State, that the
British were actually leaving Palestine, and that Jewish refugees would
have a place to go.

# 2
# The Plunge

In January 1948 it was decided that my family and I would return to New York, ostensibly to put the mill back in operation, but this was not to be. Fate began to take a hand, when after settling back into our apartment in Great Neck, I called Norm Weisman to learn the latest news of the Thursday luncheons. Norm brought me up-to-date and then relayed a rather mysterious message.

It seems that last week's speaker had been an ex-American Palestinian by the name of Victor Avrunin. After the meeting he had sought out Norm and asked if he would contact me. The message was merely that Avrunin would like to meet me and would I please give him a call.

At the time it was strange that he knew of my friendship with Norm and seemed even stranger that he wanted to meet me. Later I realized that his interest must have stemmed from a conversation I had had with Shlomo Rabinovitch-later Shamir- who had spoken at a meeting about a year before.

At that time I mentioned to Shlomo that I had served in the U.S. Navy as a ship repair officer, and would be happy to help with any naval problems. The matter had ended there, and although Norm and I later had a few dealings with Shlomo, the subject of a navy never came up.

Years later Shlomo mentioned that in those early days no one had ever considered a navy and when I had mentioned the subject he was quite shocked.

The prospect of a meeting with Avrunin was of course, most intriguing since until this time our contacts with the Materials for Palestine groups were very superficial. The following week I called Avrunin and agreed to meet him at Hotel Fourteen on East Sixtieth Street in New York.

The hotel itself seemed like a typical residential hotel, and from the lobby one certainly did not get the impression that it was a center of Jewish Palestinian activity. I found Avrunin in a tiny room that must have been a broom closet—for very small brooms. There was just room for him, a small desk, and a chair for visitors.

He was a short heavyset American with gray hair, a deep voice, and a very pleasant manner. By way of introduction he explained a bit about his own background. It seems that he had studied engineering at the University of Michigan and had gone to Palestine with his wife Judy some years before World War II. During the war he had served as a major in the Jewish Brigade of the British Army. In my mind, anybody with such a background couldn't be all bad.

During this transition period before the new state came into existence, the Jewish Agency for Palestine had begun to act on behalf of the coming Jewish State. Since it was abundantly clear that the new state would have to defend itself, an army had to be organized and equipped in but four months' time. The agency had sent Avrunin and a number of others to the United States to purchase equipment for the new army from World War II surplus stocks that were on sale in the United States.

In the course of conversation he seemed curious about my background and asked me all the appropriate questions. In essence, the fact that I had studied naval architecture and marine engineering and had been a division officer aboard a U.S. Navy repair ship—U.S.S. *Altair*—during the war, seemed to be of particular interest.

By this time, we were Vic and Hal, and we seemed to hit it off from the beginning. Actually, this was the beginning of a long and close friendship. As Vic explained, all of his purchases—with one small exception—were to be the nonmunitions items required by the new army, such things as tents, uniforms, shoes, and trucks. The "pots and pans," as he put it.

The reason for specializing in nonmunitions was due to the fact that a month before—5 December 1947—the U.S. government had imposed an embargo on military supplies to the Mideast. Thus, it was thought that by dealing only in supplies that were not included under the embargo, all sorts of problems could be avoided.

Just before leaving Palestine, however, someone had shoved a piece of paper into his hand with a list of ships required by the new navy, together with the casual request, "While you're in the United States would you pick up a fleet from war surplus?"

The need for a navy was certainly real, for Palestine was virtually surrounded by Arab countries who blatantly proclaimed their hostile intentions. This meant that the only access to the new state was by air and sea. Moreover, Egypt had an established navy that had been supplied and trained by the British.

Thus, in order to afford some protection against naval bombardment of the coast and harassment of shipping, a navy was required. Since Vic was an expert in transportation, it had been decided that his office should handle the purchase of the ships even if these might be questionable in terms of the embargo. Somehow or other, a way would have to be found to deal with the export technicalities.

Finally, Vic came to the point of our meeting and said: "Hal, I think you know more about buying ships than I do, so why not come to work with us and buy the navy?"

It was as if he had hit me in the face. I was completely shocked. Up until then, the entire struggle for a Jewish State was something you read about. You might even flit about the fringes by going to a meeting or giving a donation, but this was for real.

I must have muttered something about having a business, for Vic said, "Close it; this is more important." As I sat there I remember thinking, "He's right. This is more important." I must have then said something about what happens after I buy the ships, and he had a ready answer. "Then you'll come to Palestine and set up a navy yard to take care of the fleet."

Of course this was not the sort of issue to be resolved on the spur of the moment, so I agreed to think it over and let him know my decision in a day or two.

3

# The Decision

Well, here I was with a completely unsuspected problem on my hands, and I had to resolve it in but a day or two. For the last several years I had devoured everything written on the subject of a Jewish Homeland. My wife and I had been to all sorts of meetings and had often offered our services to local pressure groups. We had even vaguely toyed with the idea of "someday" going to Palestine. However, what Vic proposed involved immediate decisive action. Without a doubt this was the most difficult decision I ever had to make.

Because over five thousand other young men and women were being called upon to make similar decisions in those days, it might be worthwhile to explore the issues we all faced. Our world of experience was completely different and it's difficult to understand why anyone would do something considered so obviously mad by today's standards. So let us explore some of the problems through the eyes of those living through this period.

One's immediate family was of course the first problem. In my case, I had a wife and eight-month-old son to consider. Leaving a secure job to buy a Jewish fleet was not such a serious problem. However, going off to my second war and then perhaps bringing my family to the new Jewish State, with all the obvious implications, was another matter entirely.

Our families were still another consideration. My wife and I both had very close loving families with parents who truly cared. We each had a brother and sister, plus aunts and uncles and cousins, all of whom comprised a close-knit family.

The most painful part was the typical history of each family. Our grandfathers fled anti-Semitism in Eastern Europe. They came to the Golden Land—America—alone, where they worked like slaves to scrape up the fares to bring over the families they left behind.

My father started earning money at the age of seven, delivering hats for a milliner. At twelve, he left school to help support his family. Our fathers were industrious, clever, and probably lucky as well, for they

20

achieved the American dream. They lived well, moved to the suburbs, and sent their kids to the best schools.

Now this meshuggener son wanted to turn his back on all that they had achieved.

My poor father simply couldn't understand and his basic argument was: "Why you?"

This was the crux of the matter—why me? To understand this, we must understand our growing up in that wonderful free society.

When we were in elementary school my folks decided that their kids must have the best possible education. For a Jew, even in America, this was fundamental for making one's way in life. So we moved to Winnetka, Illinois, which was reputed to have the best school system.

Our schooling was superb. In addition to the three Rs, we learned about American history and democracy. We were steeped in the idealized history of our nation. We not only knew about how our predecessors fled oppression to the freedom of America, but we felt it in our kishkes.

Jefferson, Washington, Daniel Boone, and all the others, weren't just historical characters, they were as close to me as my own uncles. We were so proud of our American heritage. Yet we Jews were somehow a bit apart.

Until my navy days, I never experienced any outward anti-Semitism, but I certainly heard all about this cloud that hung over our lives. Despite my sheltered existence, anti-Semitism was an integral part of my life. Little Jewish boys and girls were taught they had to be more polite, quieter, cleaner, nicer, and above all, get higher grades in school than other kids. We knew that regardless of our schooltime fantasies about democracy, society was often anti-Semitic.

Winnetka was a Christian community and it did seem odd to me that I never received invitations to the Christmas dances but since I had, as yet, not discovered girls, this passed me by with no ill affects.

My first encounter with this problem occurred in the navy when I was about to be married. (By this time I had discovered girls.) Since my five-day leave specifically stated that I had to stay within fifty miles of Washington, D.C., I turned to a local travel agent to locate an appropriate resort. Of course a lieutenant in the navy looking for a honeymoon spot was welcomed with open arms, and I left with fifty brochures—by actual count.

Each was wonderfully attractive. How do you choose? I sat with these spread out on my bed and tried to decide. Then, for lack of a better way, I started to read the small print. My heavens! There it was, "Restricted Clientele." I sort of laughed, for I had heard of this, but never had actually come across the real thing. This started a search in the small print of the other leaflets and I found that out of the fifty, there was only one that did not specifically state, in one way or another, that Jews were not accepted.

I really don't want to overemphasize this incident, for I was more curious than hurt. It does, however, illustrate how we were one of the boys, but not one of "the boys." I'm sure any American black will understand this.

With this as a background, we lived through the rise of Hitler. We heard about Jews, people like ourselves, being rounded up and sent to concentration camps. Such stories that we heard as children about bygone days in the Russian ghettos were actually happening in our time. How could anyone raised in this American haven of freedom react to this horror? We rushed to volunteer in the war against fascism.

As time went by, we learned that the truth was far more horrible than our expectations. Millions of people—my people—were singled out and butchered like cattle, simply because they were Jews. We did hear of some heroes who tried to help, but sadly we also heard of governments and large segments of the Christian world who somehow preferred to look aside rather become involved.

This was only the beginning, however. World War II was now over and the Nazis were defeated. Why was the world unwilling to help the survivors? These pitiful remnants of Europe's Jewish community languished in concentration camps. Seven hundred thousand persecuted human wrecks had been liberated, but had no place to go. Where was this civilization of which we were so proud?

Britian made it very clear that she could not, or perhaps one should say, would not, help. Canada would not accept them. Even the United States had trouble accepting 100,000 refugees.

Since during the last months of the war I was stationed in Washington, I went to the congressional debate on allowing 100,000 Jewish refugees to enter America. Up until then, the United States had allowed only 1,447 to enter the country. The speech by Senator Owen D. Brewster (Republican Senator from Maine) truly made me proud to be an American. In the tradition of America's founding fathers, he made it clear that the United States had always prided itself on its history of welcoming the oppressed and thus must accept these Jewish refugees. On the other hand, other speakers made it abundantly clear that not everyone was as sympathetic.

One could not help reliving Herzl's thoughts during the Dreyfus trial. "There must be a Jewish State," but again the dilemma did not end there.

The United Nations had decided to partition Palestine, so theoretically there would be a Jewish State. In reality, however, it looked as if there was another Holocaust in the making.

The United Nations had declared the partition of Palestine and the British had agreed to leave, but in December 1947 they had also proclaimed that they would not hand over the administration to any other authority.

They made it clear that no militia would be allowed to maintain order as they systematically left the country. This was despite the fact that on 2 December 1947, three days after the United Nations ratified the partition plan, Achmed Sharabati, minister of national defense of Syria, called for volunteers to conquer the proposed state. Students in Syria—a member of the United Nations—would henceforth study only until noon so as to allow time for military training for the coming war.

Then, on 18 December, the Arab League Council met in Cairo. Here, their prime ministers met to discuss the forces needed to defeat the U.N. decision.

During this period, every day the newspapers contained headlines such as the following, which appeared in 1948 in the *Palestine Post*.

1 January     Haifa Massacre

1 January     Syria Passes Anti-Jewish Measures

2 January     Britain Ignores Arab's War Declaration-Ben-Gurion

4 January     Jewish Suburbs Under Fire, 6 Dead in Haifa

4 January     Ramat Gan Suburbs Under Fire

5 January     Safad Cut Off

6 January     600 Jews and Arabs Dead in 5 Weeks

This all added up to a very ominous series of conclusions: the proposed Jewish State was surrounded by enemies with established armies that had publicly declared their intentions to invade. Fighting had already broken out and not only did the British tolerate this, but they were doing all in their power to prevent the Jewish community from organizing any sort of defense. Then, to make matters even worse, the American government announced its embargo of military supplies.

Were our fears exaggerated by our overly sensitive emotions? As the year 1948 continued, we soon saw the reality of our expectations.

30 January      The British refused to allow the United Nations to enter Palestine in order to set up some sort of interim authority.

22 February     Palestine was expelled from the sterling bloc.

7 March         British ships were no longer allowed to call at Palestine ports.

7 March         Import licenses were no longer granted for any items, including food.

15 April        The refinery was closed.

1 May           Surface mail was discontinued.

19 May          The British government refused to agree to sanctions against the Arab countries that invaded Israel.

Clearly, the British activities to prevent the establishment of the Jewish State were not limited to the military. Refusal to allow the United Nations to enter and establish an interim authority insured that chaos would prevail. Expelling Palestine from the sterling bloc removed the backing from the currency. Finally, such commercial tactics as prohibiting British ships from calling at Palestine ports, discontinuing import licenses, and stopping the mails were obviously meant to cause a collapse of the economy.

No, history shows that we did not exaggerate the danger. Who would help this beleaguered people? Only the people of whom I was somehow a part, the Jews. Over five thousand young Jews, mostly war veterans from all over the world, felt the same as I. They answered their father's questions: "Why you?" with the only rational reply: "Who else?"

Still a mad decision, but perhaps more understandable. My wife and I agreed that it was the thing to do. My father said something I can never forget. "I don't really understand why you must do this, but I respect your decision. Just remember, if things don't work out, you have a father."

# 4
# Commitment

Five minutes after reporting to work I was in the midst of my first crisis. "How would you store a country's fuel without a proper tank farm?" All of Palestine's fuel storage facilities were in the Haifa Bay area near the refinery, and if the area fell to the Arabs there would literally be no place to store fuel in the entire country.

In those days, the lower town of Haifa around the port was in Arab hands, with the Jewish residential areas on Mount Carmel above the lower city. This meant that each day several thousand Jewish workers in buses and trucks had to go through the Arab town to get to and from work. Already at this early date this was a very dangerous journey with sniping all the way.

Then, on 31 December 1947, the Arab workers in the refinery went berserk, killing thirty-nine Jews, and the refinery had to be closed. Hence, the fuel storage problem was very ominous and took precedence over buying navies.

Someone gave me a report of an American plan, apparently developed in World War II, for emergency fuel storage. Essentially, the proposal suggested digging artificial lakes, lining these with some impervious material, and then flooding the lakes with fuel.

Vic had called in a couple of other engineers and we wrestled with "What does one do with the thousands of tons of fuel needed by an entire country at war?" To make things even more bizzare, Vic was in the midst of a kidney stone attack. Each time he would be seized with pain we would all insist on bringing in a doctor, but he would mutter, "Keep going, we've got to finish this."

Finally, a doctor was called, but the crisis and the stone seemed to pass about the same time. No one ever mentioned why the fuel crisis was over, but we turned to other problems.

Vic had managed to obtain a small office and staff of three or four specialists. Ben Adleman—later Eden—was a Canadian who like Vic, had settled in Palestine and had also been a major in the Jewish Brigade. Theodore Hertzl Rome—that really was his name—was American, a fine artist, but more important, he was managing his family's surplus business. When he had seen the magnitude of Vic's purchasing program, he volunteered to help locate the various items on the shopping list.

Since everything was just beginning, Vic had some very basic decisions to make and he truly showed a great understanding of the issues. Moreover, he made the required decisions without hesitation.

Until this time, supplies had been sent in small quantities on merchant ships, which stopped at all sorts of ports on a given route. Since things were heating up in the area, shipping companies were already writing "war clauses" into their contracts. They all seemed to feel that if there was any damage they could drop the cargo destined for Palestine off at the nearest port—Beirut.

The obvious solution was to charter entire ships and this required a private pier and warehouse. Having so decided, Vic made the necessary arrangements and the ink was hardly dry before the shrieking started. "Delusions of grandeur, how could he undertake such steps on our microbudget?"

As Vic explained, we were not merchants. We were a government—even though the state had yet to be declared—and it was high time we started behaving like a government. Of course he was right, but the budget problems of the critics had to be faced.

This chronic lack of funds led to some very far-reaching and strange decisions. The money available simply was not enough to equip an entire army. So it was decided to buy used equipment and uniforms from U.S. war surplus.

"You expect our boys to wear someone's old clothes and boots?" "You're going to fight a war with broken-down trucks that have already been through World War II?"

The answer was, "Yes, we have no other alternative." Actually, much of the equipment had been repaired and put into reasonably good condition. The army boots had all been resoled and the uniforms laundered and patched.

While still stinging from the numerous critics, Vic invited Mickey Marcus up to the office to get a real expert's opinion. Mickey was indeed an expert: West Point graduate; colonel in the American Army; and most important, an American volunteer in the Israeli Army. He did what he thought was right and early in June of 1948 he paid with his life.

Marcus was certainly a dynamic person; he literally glowed with vitality. When Vic explained the issue, he whipped off his jacket, tie, and shirt, and tried on one of the used shirts. He went through some calisthenics and then turned to Vic and said, "This is fine; don't let them talk you out of it."

Vehicles, mainly jeeps and trucks, were a far more complex issue. Most war surplus vehicles needed some sort of overhaul and the picture was further complicated by the need to disassemble them in order to cram the maximum number of vehicles into a ship. Again the approach was realistic but somewhat unsuspected. We would buy the used vehicles and send these to Palestine. There, one of the old British workshops would be put back into operation, reconditioning the "new" vehicles. Again there were screams of criticism and Vic later mentioned that there was even talk of a lynching when the first trucks were unloaded. They looked like junk.

According to Vic's account later, when Ben Gurion saw these used disassembled vehicles being unloaded he moaned: "This is what he did with our money?" Actually, the program was completely sound, and in the end, things worked out exactly as planned. The vehicle program was my first professional task, for someone had to figure out how many trucks one could actually load into the chartered ship.

It was about this time that Judy Avrunin—Vic's wife—received a shock. Judy was the Haifa representative of the *Palestine Post*—the local English newspaper. She had remained behind when Vic had gone off to the United States.

One day one of Judy's contacts with the Hagana came to see her in her office and out of the blue said, "Get packed; you're going to the States." She of course was shocked, but it was explained that Vic was afraid that as communications collapsed they would be cut off from each other. He had insisted that either Judy came to him or he was going back since he would not leave her alone. The Hagana representative explained that Vic's mission was so important that she was to leave immediately.

Hotel Fourteen was literally a beehive of Palestinian activity. However, the various projects were compartmentalized. Hence, it was only years later that I learned what other machinations were really going on around me in those days. We did know a few of the people in offices that dealt with our projects, but more or less concerned ourselves with our own problems, such as buying a navy.

# 5

# Buying a Navy

Vic's list of ships was short and simple: 3 PCs (patrol crafts), 3 SCs (submarine chasers), and 3 MTBs (motor torpedo boats), and 2 LCIs (landing craft-infantry), and 1 sea going tug. Their specifications are listed in the following table, together with the specifications of the key ships of the Egyptian Navy at that time.

All of these vessels were classified as "small craft" by the U.S. Navy and if one realized that destroyers of World War II were ships of 2,100 or 2,200 tons, one can see why the PCs of 295 tons were considered small. Actually, the PCs and SCs were used as patrol and antisubmarine vessels carrying only very light armament.

The MTBs did carry torpedoes that certainly are serious weapons, but torpedoes require very elaborate maintenance and training facilities far beyond the scope of a new navy, yet to be established.

Thus, at best, the proposed navy was a very modest affair. However, purchasing the ships was but a small beginning to a very complex chain of events. First, the ships available on the market had been stripped of everything even remotely military. Somehow the military hardware would have to be obtained somewhere else, for in the United States—the logical source—there was the embargo.

Next in the series of events was to bring these hulks back to functioning warships and integrate the newfound equipment. Presumably this second phase would take place in Israel.

Finally, crews would have to be trained to sail the ships and this, even in the United States, with proper training facilities, was a long and difficult task. Consequently, building this very modest naval fleet was a most complicated task, to be finished in but a few months.

In contrast, the Egyptian Navy was established and had been supplied and trained by the British. The table lists their key ships and, although their navy was not in the big leagues unopposed, it could do considerable damage to shipping, coastal cities, and the new Jewish Navy.

The purchase of this mininavy was the easiest part of the program. The U.S. government had dumped hundreds of such ships on the

### Egyptian Fleet

| Type | Tons | Speed | Armament | Number | Name |
|---|---|---|---|---|---|
| Destroyer | 1,105 | 16 | 2 4," 2 37 mm | 1 | Ex-HMS Fowey |
| Sloop | 1,440 | 17 | 1 6" | 1 | Farouk |
| Sloop | 2,640 | 14 | 2 3 1b. | 1 | Fawzia |
| Corvette | 1,290 | 16 | 1 6 1b. | 1 | . . . |
| BYMS | 215 | 13 | 1 3," 2 20 mm | 8 | . . . |
| ML | 65 | 19 | 1 3 1b., 3 20 mm | 1 | . . . |

### Israeli Navy to Be Purchased

| | | | | | |
|---|---|---|---|---|---|
| PC | 295 | 13 | . . . | 3 | . . . |
| SC | 50 | . . . | . . . | 3 | . . . |
| MTB | 62 | . . . | . . . | 3 | . . . |
| LCI | . . . | . . . | . . . | 2 | . . . |
| Tug | . . . | . . . | . . . | 1 | . . . |

### Israeli Navy-Actual

| | | | | | |
|---|---|---|---|---|---|
| Corvette | 925 | 13 | . . . | 2 | Wedgewood K18 |
| | | | | | Hagana K20 |
| Ice Breaker | 2,050 | 8 | . . . | 1 | Eilat |
| Yacht | . . . | 18 | . . . | 1 | Maox K24 |
| SC | . . . | . . . | . . . | 2 | Dror |
| | | | | | Tirtzah |
| ML | . . . | . . . | . . . | 1 | Portzeme |
| Landing Craft | . . . | . . . | . . . | | |
| PC | 295 | 20 | . . . | 1 | Nogah |

market for anyone to buy. Most went to scrap yards, but some purchasers used the ships for commercial purposes. Others converted naval vessels into pleasure yachts. Some foreign governments bought very cheap additions to their navies.

Our central problem was not finding available ships; it was how to arrange their export. Ships have a national identity and carry the flag of the nation of registry. Changing from one flag to another is a legal problem requiring cooperation of the country of registry, namely, the United States, in this case.

To be sure, such changes in flag were made all the time. In fact, the papers carried stories of Arab nations buying these ex-warships with the full cooperation of the U.S. government. In fact, the Saudis had recently bought an LCI for commercial use, as they put it, and there were no problems. We, however, had problems.

On the preceding December 5 an embargo of military supplies to the Mideast had been declared and whereas Saudi Arabia could buy war surplus ships, the coming Jewish State was definitely not allowed this same right.

No one had any idea of how we would deal with the situation, so it was decided that Hal should locate the appropriate vessels and make the necessary down payments until the problem could be resolved.

Even this was much too simple; there had to be another catch. The preceding month some boxes of machinery being loaded for Palestine in New York, broke open, revealing a very strange type of machinery that strongly resembled TNT. Of course all activity on the pier stopped and the entire shipment was impounded. To make matters worse, the FBI began to take a very special interest in the Jewish agency, its people, and offices.

Thus, whereas Vic's office openly worked on nonembargo items, my work had to be strictly secret. No phone calls from the office or from home. No contacts that could be traced to the office and no records.

This meant that for the next few months I carried a pocketful of dimes for public phones. I came to know all the phone booths in the area and in a sense these became my office. The vital statistics of the various vessels that had to be recorded were written in a small note-book in speedwriting. This is a shorthand system that was better than any code since even I had trouble understanding my own notes.

My first visit to a shipyard revealed yet another problem. Three MTBs—motor torpedo boats—were advertised in the paper and I went to check them out at the Flushing Meadows Marina. After climbing all over them and squeezing through all the bilges and around the engines, the owner and I started to talk business.

Suddenly he asked: "What did you say your name was?" I was momentarily stumped since I obviously could not use my own name and hadn't thought to prepare something suitable. A good Christian name was needed right then and the only thing that popped into my mind was "Skinhead Jenkins," one of my chief petty officers from the U.S.S. *Altair*. So for the moment I became Jenkins.

At home, however, this precipitated still another problem since my wife jokingly informed me that I could be Mr. Jenkins if I liked, but she was not going to be Mrs. Jenkins. So I asked her to pick a name and next time I would be prepared. After some thought she decided that since I was blond with blue eyes I looked like an Anderson, so Anderson it was.

Actually, locating a ship and arranging the purchase was quite simple. There were dozens of each type available and most were quite new. Since the majority were destined for the scrap yard, prices were low and pretty uniform. One ship was even a gift.

One morning Vic mentioned that he had received a call from someone who wanted to give us a PC-170 foot patrol craft—but he had no idea who the man was. He did have a phone number and a name.

On calling the number a woman told me that her husband had made the call and indeed had a ship that he wanted to give us. We agreed that it would be better for me to come to see them and she gave me directions to their home near Vineland, New Jersey. Vineland should have been the "tip-off," for this area was settled by Jewish farmers in the 1880s.

Sure enough, as I approached the area where they lived, I noticed large prosperous farms, but the most interesting feature was the names on the mailboxes. Goldberg, Cohen, Ginsberg, Minkovitch, and all sorts of obviously Jewish names, but hardly a place for a man with a warship. When I finally located the house it was that of Mr. Jacobson, a carpenter.

After we had introduced ourselves, he explained that he really did have a ship for us. It seems that one of the Jews of the neighborhood was in the scrap business and he and his Christian partner had bought a PC to cut up for the steel scrap. The ship was in excellent condition and when his Jewish friends heard about it, they decided that they would buy out the partner and give the ship to the new Jewish State. The scrap yard was not far, and sure enough, it was a beautiful PC with a wonderful price.

This was indeed an inspiring phenomenon. Here we had prosperous farmers who had lived in the area for two generations. Good solid Americans with perhaps one strange feature. They were Jews and herein exhibited a characteristic we were to see over and over again.

They identified with fellow Jews who suffered in Europe and wanted to help. Donating money did not seem to be enough. They wanted to do something more tangible, like give their own personal warship.

We were to see this phenomenon over and over again. Much of the equipment Vic located was owned by Jews and in many cases they donated what they had or made it available at sacrifice prices.

One case of this compulsion to help, particularly pertinent to our ships, occurred one night. We had been struggling with the problem of how to transfer the flags of the fleet I had assembled and an interesting idea evolved.

Why not have Christian friends in South America buy the ships for "commercial purposes" and transfer the flags to their home countries?

This was done all the time with no particular problems. Arab states were also doing this without difficulty.

After the ships were safely registered in South America, they could easily be transferred to the Jewish State. If all else failed, we could do this last transfer for a price. In South America the approach to such business was not unknown. To make it even more interesting, we had a close friend from the Thursday luncheons who did business in South America.

It was midnight, but the new state was due in a matter of weeks, so out I went to a phone booth and called. Our friend had been asleep, but when he heard who it was and learned that I wanted to see him right away, he immediately said, "Come on over; I'll be waiting for you."

When I got to his apartment he was in pajamas and a robe but by now quite wide awake. He wouldn't listen to an apology; he understood the urgency.

He heard what we had in mind, thought a moment, and said, "I think this could work; I do have the right contacts in several countries. However, I'm ill and travel would be a problem." He paused and then continued. "I'll tell you what; suppose I go to only two countries to see if we can do the whole job from just two."

I, of course, was thrilled and very timidly asked: "When do you think you could make the trip?" He then replied: "Would tomorrow be OK?" Such people made life worth living.

The following morning I sat down with our lawyers, but they were reticent to try this and felt that we could find a way to get permission from the U.S. government. At one point, in desperation, I threw out the suggestion: "Why don't we simply sail the ships to Palestine and run up our own flag—who would know?" Whereupon I received his most disapproving legal stare together with: "Son, do you want to go to jail for twenty years? What you've just suggested is piracy."

# 6
# Winding Up the Office

Well it finally happened. Friday, 14 May 1948, as I drove home from work listening to the news, it was announced that the State of Israel had been proclaimed. Moreover, President Truman had recognized the new state. I was so excited I almost drove off the parkway. How can one explain almost forty years later what we felt? Here was an American boy born of American parents whose only real contact with his heritage was marginal and most assuredly superficial, but there on the Belt Parkway I felt unbounded joy.

It was not until early June that the lawyers and politicians came to some sort of an agreement. Vic informed me that Admiral Howard Leroy Vickery of the U.S. Maritime Commission, had finally agreed to accept the ships as commercial vessels, the same as for any other country. Our lawyer was due to call in awhile to get the ship numbers, types, and locations so as to start the transfer process.

Now up until this time no one, not even Vic, knew these particulars. There were no records and certainly no discussions of such information; it was strictly secret.

Suddenly, the phone rang and Vic turned the call over to me with a word of explanation; this was the lawyer who needed the information. To my amazement I couldn't talk. I was so steeped in secrecy that I literally sat there like a dummy and the words would not come out. The lawyer kept saying, "Come on, give me the information," and I kept telling myself, "Gershenow, you're behaving like a damned idiot. Tell him what he wants to know," but the words wouldn't come.

Finally, with enormous difficulty, I managed to give him the data and in a sense this phase of my work was over.

It was only several months later in Israel that I heard what finally happened. Apparently, after receiving the information, the Maritime Commission sat on it for a while and then changed their minds leaving us without our navy. Such betrayals are all part of one's personal and nation's experience. Today, when Israel is sometimes reluctant to go along with our good friends from overseas, I realize that such experiences helped to shape the nation's diplomacy.

Having completed most of our purchases, work in the United States was grinding to a halt, but all sorts of odds and ends had to be handled.

One small job that is particularly interesting in the light of subsequent events and history, had to do with five thousand Czech pistols in the free port of New York. Someone found his way to Vic with this offer that was hard to refuse.

A free port is exactly what its name implies. Goods in the New York free port do not come under the jurisdiction of the U.S. government. Hence, the embargo did not apply to these pistols and the owner was free to ship these anywhere he liked.

The original owner of the pistols was told that we did not deal in such items, but someone would probably contact him. The matter was then given to me to convey to Teddy Kolleck. Today, of course, Teddy is the famous mayor of Jerusalem; however, I found him then in a grubby little hotel room where we sat on the bed because the tiny room had no chairs.

Much of the American Jewish community by this time was either aware or actually caught up in activities of the new Jewish State; one evening my father seemed very much involved. He called me at home and his first words were, "Harold, I have something for you." From the stilted tone of his voice I could literally see him holding at arm's length with two fingers, a pistol.

Before he could say another word, I interrupted and said, "Dad, I'll be right over." Sure enough he had the largest 45-caliber revolver I'd ever seen. It was straight out of the Wild West. Apparently, one of his friends had dropped over with a package and a hurried comment that Harold would know what to do with it.

Toward the end of May we began to close up our office in Hotel Fourteen. Much of the army's equipment had been shipped, the transfer of flags of the navy vessels was ostensibly being processed, and Vic and Judy were to return to Israel on June 13.

Vic had suggested that I make my preparations to leave and he would make the necessary arrangements in Israel. According to plan, this would take about two weeks and the staff at Hotel Fourteen were to send me off to Israel as soon as word from Vic arrived.

I needed a passport, and here I got the first of many little shocks. After filling out the application and submitting this to the clerk, he looked me in the eye and said: "You realize that volunteering in a foreign military service is against the law?" I never did figure out if he could read minds or if this was routine.

My wife and I had decided that she and fifteen-month-old David would move in with my in-laws. Since my parents and in-laws lived only about seventy-five yards apart in Great Neck, and there was no shortage of room at either house, this was an ideal temporary measure.

We were busy arranging all sorts of details; sandwiched in this array of activities was a small medical operation, convalescence, and a five-day vacation.

After a couple of weeks there had been no word from Vic about my coming to Israel and no one at Hotel Fourteen seemed to know quite what to do. I was soon to find that this was par for the course. Finally, it was decided to wait until "Admiral" Yossie Hamburger—Harel—arrived and put the problem up to him. Since he was due in a few days this seemed to be the best solution.

A few days later I got a call that the admiral had arrived, the next day we met at Hotel Fourteen. He was a tall good-looking young man about my age—twenty-six. He seemed pretty young for an admiral, but he might have thought that I was young to be the prospective head of Israel's Navy Yard. There didn't seem to be an unoccupied corner for us at the hotel so us seadogs went down the street to a bar for our meeting—where else? Over our Coca Colas we discussed the various aspects of our problem.

Yossie must have been well briefed, for he seemed to know all about me. After a general review of the issues he changed course and began to paint a pretty grim picture of the situation in Israel. He made it very clear that he could not guarantee my safety, for no one had any idea how the military situation would develop. Living conditions were also a problem and he made it very clear that he could not guarantee me a decent place to sleep or enough to eat.

Finally, Yossie explained that although I probably knew more about maintaining a navy than most of those I would come across in Israel, the local experts would never admit it. Moreover, he assured me that all sorts of people would be after my job or at least try to tell me how to run things. After painting this very grim picture he suddenly asked: "Are you really sure you want to go?"

I've often thought that Yossie's approach was certainly very mature and fair. I truly appreciated his trying to give me every bit of background and every possibility to back out.

His appraisal of the military situation was no surprise since we read about air raids. We also knew that although there was a cease-fire on June 2, the fighting had started up again on June 9. We at Hotel Fourteen also knew how ill prepared for a war with established armies Israel really was.

I cannot imagine why, but I must have said yes, for Yossie then smiled and said, "It's really not as bad as I painted it. Let's go back to the hotel and make the arrangements."

There really was not much to arrange. One seat was available on the following Tuesday the twentieth—to Paris via Air France with a connecting flight to Israel. After arranging this, I was asked to go out and buy a new tube of my usual shaving cream. A short while later it was returned to me with instructions to deliver it to the naval authorities on my arrival. I was then instructed to be at the Air France office in Manhattan at 3:00 A.M. Monday, where someone would meet me with tickets and all the necessary documents.

This left only one outstanding problem. According to U.S. naval regulations, a reserve officer, even after his discharge from active duty, cannot leave the United States without obtaining permission. In those days, it must be remembered, people did not go abroad as today. A trip to Europe was a major journey and one to Israel was unheard-of. Going off to join a foreign navy was also highly illegal and even going off to work abroad was bound to involve all sorts of potentially awkward discussions.

What to do? After long and careful thought I decided to write the necessary letter requesting permission to leave the country and to mail it a day or two before leaving. A friend, Eddie Mendel, who was in the importing business, offered to make me his European representative. Thus my request gave not only an ostensibly rational reason, but an established American firm as my employer.

Since I was to leave the country on Tuesday the twentieth, I mailed the letter on Monday the nineteenth. However, I was really due for a shock. Monday afternoon I received a call from Hotel Fourteen informing me that my ticket was needed for some VIP and I would not leave until Thursday the twenty-second. Of course I had all sorts of recriminations about mailing the navy letter so soon but, after a little thought, I realized that a letter mailed on Monday could hardly be delivered and find its way through the bureaucracy by Thursday morning.

However, around noon on Wednesday, Eddie called with a rather unpleasant message. During the morning there had been half a dozen calls for Harold Gershenow and, each time the secretary said that he was not in, the caller simply hung up. All of this was very mysterious, for we thought that only Eddie, his secretary, and I knew about our arrangement.

Finally, on the next call Eddie picked up the phone, introduced himself, and asked for an explanation. The caller then identified himself as a commander in Naval Intelligence and demanded to know my whereabouts. Without hesitating, Eddie declared that his business was a highly competitive one and he was not about to discuss his employee's whereabouts with someone who "claimed" to be a commander in the navy.

Whereupon the voice said, "Have Gershenow call me at the Third Naval District Headquarters as soon as he arrives." Of course Eddie was as concerned as I.

One must realize that had it not been for all the secrecy of the past few months and for all the concern as to what the various agencies actually knew about our activities, I would not have been very worried. Under the circumstances, however, I was very much concerned.

What to do, however, was another matter. Actually, there was very little to do but shove off and hope for the best. So it was decided that I had left before Eddie had been able to reach me and I had not received the message.

Thursday morning my friend Marvin Chaiken drove me to New York and dropped me off at Air France where I was to meet the boys from Hotel Fourteen. Over my shoulder I carried a large camera case that later turned out to be a very important asset during the trip. In my suitcase was my entire wardrobe plus tools of the trade—a carefully selected technical library, a slide rule, and drawing instruments.

While waiting for my contacts from the hotel I shrunk into the background worrying that each stranger coming into Air France was from Naval Intelligence out to pick me up. However, nothing of the sort occurred and in a few minutes my friends appeared lugging two huge and obviously heavy duffle bags.

They explained that the duffle bags were the diplomatic mail that I was taking to Israel. Israel then was a very young state with no procedures for such matters, so whoever was going, took the mail.

After giving me two separate tickets, one to Paris and another from Paris to Israel, I was also handed a series of envelopes each with an explanation. "This must be delivered in Paris in person; keep it on your person at all times. This should be delivered to the naval authorities; it's most secret. Do not let it off your person. This is your letter of introduction to the navy. Hide it on your person." They certainly seemed to want personal service.

With so much to be secreted on my body I began to wonder if I should have borrowed a suit from my father who was several sizes larger than I.

Following the check in process and the best wishes for a good trip and the appropriate *shalom*, I was on my way. At Idlewild—now Kennedy—the check in was also very straightforward and as I buckled my seat belt I could not help but feel a sense of relief from the worries of the past weeks and anticipation of an entirely new life. This is really what happened.

# 7
# The Flight

My pleasant reverie was due for a shock, for after but a few minutes the stewardess asked everyone to fasten their seat belts for landing. My first reaction was that Naval Intelligence had finally caught up with me. However, on questioning the stewardess I learned that this was a routine stop at Boston for passengers and fuel. The plane was a World War II Constellation and hadn't the range of today's airliners, so we were due to make a number of such stops before reaching Paris.

At Boston the passengers were all herded into a transit lounge and there we began to meet one another. There were a number of young fellows on the plane and we began discussing our plans for Paris. One was on his way to study at the Sorbonne, and another was off on a European vacation. Several others were going on business.

One small group of somewhat older passengers were actually on their way to Israel. Among this Israeli-bound group was Marie Syrkin who had written *Blessed Is the Match*, on the Holocaust. It turned out that we were seated just across the aisle from each other and we spent a number of hours conversing during the trip.

After a number of stops for fuel we finally arrived in Paris and as we were getting ready to disembark, I mentioned to Ms. Syrkin that I was so impressed by our conversation that I'd decided to continue on to Israel. Moreover, by some strange accident of fate I had a ticket from Paris to Israel in my pocket.

Whereupon, all of the young men who had been going to Paris on vacation and to work exclaimed, "That's strange; I have an extra ticket to Israel too; I'll join you." After a good laugh we decided to spend the few hours layover in Paris seeing the city together. One of the boys had been stationed in Paris during the latter part of the war and he offered to show us the town.

In those days, passengers on such a long trip were put up at a hotel for their stay where they could rest for a few hours. Being anxious to see the sights, we washed up and were on our way. After delivering my letter we were off to the Eifel Tower and had a lovely few hours sightseeing before returning to the terminal.

The second lap of the trip was on North African Airways, a subsidiary of Air France, since most airlines refused to fly to Israel. This time, the plane was a DC3. Since the range of the DC3 was very limited, we spent almost as much time going up and down for fuel as we did going forward.

Nice, Bari, Athens, and Cyprus were all stops along the way and with time the conditions aboard the plane deteriorated as we progressed. By the time we reached Cyprus there was no drinking water left on the plane; things were pretty foul in the washrooms; and we were all hot, sweaty, and tired.

Cyprus was about as primitive as one could expect. The terminal was a broken-down Quonset hut with torn screens, buzzing with flies and various British officials. After we had again boarded, Marie Syrkin turned to me and said, "We were kind of worried that you wouldn't make it." It seems that they had overheard some of the British officials discussing whether or not to detain me. Finally, however, they decided that with such an impressive camera case I must be a news photographer. Had they inspected the case's contents they would have found a thirty-five-dollar Argus camera.

The whole idea of detaining passengers on the way to Israel had never occurred to me. By what right could they do such a thing? Apparently, the British made their own rules. Later, I learned that just two days before, they had pulled eight young Jews from a similar flight. They would not allow them to continue to Israel and gave them the alternatives of going back to Marseilles or being interned in a refugee camp.

The final leg of our journey to Haifa was quite short. Lod, Israel's main airport, was still under fire, so Haifa's little airstrip was used. As we approached the coast everyone crowded to the little windows and we were welcomed with some exciting views. First, as we circled we saw the refineries. Then, just before landing, we flew over the port where several gray ships were tied up. The color meant navy, but there were no guns visible.

The most important sight for me was a very quick glimpse of cranes. Seeing that there were cranes in the port made my day complete, for this had been one of my biggest concerns. Ship repair is virtually synonymous with lifting heavy weights, thus, cranes are mandatory. For weeks I had been worrying what we'd do if there were none available. All sorts of alternate plans had been imagined, but not any one of these was very practical. Suddenly, however, the problem was resolved. Haifa Port seemed to be well equipped.

Moments later we were on the ground and had taxied up to the terminal, a small but trim building. In those days the plane parked about fifty yards from the terminal and everyone walked to the building.

As we approached the terminal a short round woman carrying a tray of glasses of orange juice met us with a big smile and, "Sholom, welcome to Israel. Have a glass of Israeli orange juice." I've often thought that whatever the cost it would be worthwhile even today. Truly like coming home.

A moment later, a middle-aged man with bushy red hair in khaki shorts and shirt and knee socks approached me and asked: "Are you looking for someone?" When I answered yes, he said, "I'm the guy." Letter number two, dutifully kept on my person, went to him.

After glancing at the letter he told me that the main road to Tel Aviv was under fire from Arabs occupying villages along Mount Carmel that parallels the road. Since the road was closed, he suggested putting me in the Seaman's House in Haifa until the next morning when perhaps the situation would be better.

My reaction was typical of an American tourist. "I can't stay here tonight; I must get to Tel Aviv immediately." Somehow or other I expected him to arrange things. When I explained that I was also a postman with all sorts of special delivery mail, he suddenly called "Koppel!"

Then straight out of the movies came this Jewish cowboy. Tall, lean, brown from the sun, and hanging low on his hip was a very impressive pistol. He really had style. The pistol was in a canvas holster with a lanyard—like the Canadian Mounties wear over their shoulders—but his was wound around the holster.

As Koppel approached, my host apparently mentioned something to the effect that this nut has to get to Tel Aviv. At this point several other passengers crowded around saying they wanted to go too. Koppel agreed to take us, and after loading the baggage into and onto his prewar seven-passenger Chrysler, we were on our way.

As we left the airport, every ex-navy man would have known that one should turn right to get to Tel Aviv, but Koppel turned left. Fortunately, I kept my mouth shut and let him do the navigating. Had the main road been open we would indeed have gone right, but that night we went through the back roads. Instead of going south along the western slopes of Mount Carmel, we went south along the eastern slopes.

By this time it was getting dark and I noticed that Koppel was doing some sort of calisthenics in the front seat. First, he unwound the lanyard from around the holster, and then he slipped the lanyard over his head and shoulder. Then he removed the pistol from the holster and placed it carefully on the seat beside him. I naively guessed that it was heavy and he was making himself comfortable.

The car was blacked out, as were the few houses we could make out along the way. Occasionally we could see shadows of people flitting across the road as we passed. The younger generation in the car discussed American pop music and in due course I, the only American in the car, was asked to give a rendition of "Nature Boy," the latest American craze. My rendition must have had a sobering effect, for everyone quieted down and we sat in silent darkness until we had cut through one of the Wadis to the coast and arrived in Hadera.

At this time everyone but the meshuggener American let out a very audible sigh of relief, for we were now safely in "Jewish territory."

Customs change with time, but in those days a journey between Haifa and Tel Aviv—about seventy-five miles—began with the rustling of paper immediately on setting out. Everyone opened their sandwiches and began to eat. Halfway to one's destination was a stop—for us, Hadera—for a drink and visit to the lavatory. This we all welcomed.

As we got out of the car to enter the blacked out roadhouse, I got my next shock, but this was really a good one. Koppel was wearing a bandolier of hand grenades. New York was never like this.

We all went through the formalities of a visit to the lavatory and a bottle of orange juice, and off we went to complete the journey. As we entered Tel Aviv, Kopel asked everyone their destination at this hour— it was around 1:00 in the morning. They all wanted to go home. "Naval Headquarters? I didn't know we had one." So everyone was safely delivered and I got into the front seat and Koppel began to hunt for Naval Headquarters.

On the way I very timidly asked: "What's all this armament you're carrying?" Whereupon he looked at me like I was mad and replied: "They shoot at cars along the road; didn't you know?" When I said that nobody had shot at us, he replied, "You were lucky; last night they shot at us."

Finally, we found the place—the ex-San Remo Hotel located on the seafront. We got out and approached the hotel to find a sentry seated across the doorway with a Sten gun in his lap, sound asleep. After an appropriate apology for disturbing his rest, he trotted off to bring the duty officer who in due course appeared. He was dressed but barefoot and had obviously been asleep as well.

Fortunately, he spoke excellent English and took charge. The diplomatic mail was accepted, plus secret letter number three, and I suddenly felt much lighter. Then he got his car and drove me to the

American House Hotel. This was typical of many European hotels in that the street entrance was merely a stairway to the second floor where there was a very modest reception desk and lobby. After registering, I was shown to a small room with four cots, three of which were occupied. Within minutes the room was quiet with four sleeping guests.

# 8
# The Military Situation

The next three months were a bit of a nightmare with a whole jumble of activities going on at the same time. We were starting from the very beginning to organize a navy, recruit personnel, locate equipment, and despite the fact that we were not in a condition to operate as a navy, ships were required to undertake various missions. Finally, this seething jumble of activity was played before a backdrop of a very confused political situation.

Judging by today's conditions, we must have been considered completely mad. Vital decisions were made on the spur of the moment in street corner meetings. Rarely did we have all the facts or the time to properly consider the alternatives. In most cases, we had no alternatives.

In order to bring the reader into this chaotic picture, I will discuss the various aspects one at a time. It should be realized, however, that many of the events described in the coming chapters were really happening at the same time. First, let us consider the military situation.

A truce—the second one—had been agreed upon on the nineteenth of July, but this certainly did not mean that there were no hostilities. Each day during those months of 1948 we read headlines such as:

| | |
|---|---|
| 30 June | Arabs Block Water Supply [to Jerusalem] |
| 13 August | Arabs Blow Up Latrun Pumping Station |
| 16 September | 10-Hour Battle in Galilee |
| 20 September | 3-Hour Attack in Jerusalem |
| 20 September | Arabs Active on Central Front |
| 23 September | Legion Troops Murder 4 |

The first two headlines had a very special meaning to the Israeli population that foreigners could not have appreciated. Moreover, this one incident can help explain how some basic national attitudes began to develop.

Jerusalem has no natural water supply and the one pumping station at Latrun furnished all of the city's water. Thus, for the city to survive, this position had to be held at all costs. One must realize that Jerusalem is the center of the universe to the Jewish people; hence, insuring the safety of Jerusalem had all the overtones of a holy mission.

The station itself was surrounded by Arab forces, but the Haganah was firmly entrenched at the pumping station. The United Nations, however, felt that this tiny enclave of Jewish forces surrounded by Arabs was somehow an affront to the Arabs to be avoided if at all possible.

Since the United Nations was most anxious to resolve this delicate problem, they suggested that if the Israeli forces would vacate the place, they, the United Nations, would guarantee the pumping station's security and a continuous supply of water to Jerusalem. In those days, one stood in awe of the United Nations and such promises were felt to be like the word of God. The Israeli government accepted the offer and turned the Latrun pumping station over to the United Nation.

Unfortunately, the Arabs then moved in and blew up the pumping station and the fait accompli could not be rectified. The machinery required to supply water to a whole city could not be replaced on the spur of the moment, even for the mighty United Nations. Like so many other cases since then, the world powers simply did nothing. So much for trust in the United Nations; one can understand why subsequent governments have been reluctant to place their faith in third parties.

However, there was a much more interesting lesson to be learned. Over a year before this event, such an eventuality had been foreseen and unknown to the outside world, action had been taken to make sure that the city could survive even without Latrun. Years ago every home in Jerusalem was built over a cistern for storing rainwater. During the rainy winters water drained from the roofs and filled the cisterns, and in historic times this was actually the source of water for the city.

This system had not been used in recent times since the pipeline and pumping station were a much more practical solution to the problem. However, the town fathers very wisely decided that the old cisterns should be quietly repaired, filled, and sealed in case of an emergency. Thus, when the pumping station was destroyed, there was certainly no abundance of water, but there was enough to survive, and survival seems to be a Jewish talent.

The water in the cisterns was considered community property to be distributed only by the city. Virtually overnight, wagons with tanks of water were wheeled through the various neighborhoods each day where the residents queued with buckets to receive their daily allotment.

Under every sink in Jerusalem was a bucket and people learned to use water several times. For instance, water in which one had washed was collected in the bucket below the sink and once each day the toilet was flushed with this water. It was not easy, but Jerusalem survived and national attitudes of independence were being formed.

Actually, the truce only meant that no major military campaigns were in progress. Thus, all branches of the security forces took advantage of the respite to begin organizing a real army. It must be remembered that the state had been in existence for only ten weeks and during much of this period there had been an all-out war. There had been only eleven days during which time there was access to a full-fledged port for importing heavy equipment.

Not long before—on 11 June—Benny Adleman's two hundred forty trucks from Panama arrived in Haifa Port and the British refused to let the ship unload. Israel was a sovereign state and Haifa was its only port, but the British were then still in control of the port and made their own rules.

Finally, on 30 June the British left their last enclave in Palestine, Haifa Port. There was no turnover of authority to the new administration. All civil services were simply cut off. The country had been invaded by five member nations of the United Nations, three of whom were closely allied with the British.

Despite the frantic efforts of the new Israeli State to establish military forces for defense of the new country, the British not only refused to cooperate in the transfer of authority, but did all in their power to speed the collapse of the new nation.

Bad as the situation was with the army and civil administration, the navy was far behind the rest of the other services. A civilian head of the navy, Gershon Zac, had only been appointed on 17 March, four months before my arrival. The very late action to establish the navy was for a very sound reason. Ben Gurion and all of his advisors saw the importance of a navy. As they put it, the sea was Israel's only window to the rest of the world. Furthermore, the danger from foreign fleets was quite obvious. The problem was that the British remained in Haifa Port until 30 June. This meant that no outwardly obvious steps to develop a fleet could be taken until this date.

As Ben Gurion so wisely put it, you can't hide a navy in a "slick"— hidden cache of arms—as had been done with the army's supplies during the British Mandate. It was known that Vic was purchasing a fleet from U.S. war surplus. However, if and when this fleet would arrive was another matter. The need was immediate and something had to be done to satisfy the need then and there. The one faint ray of hope was in Haifa Port.

Along the breakwater of Haifa Port were several dozen refugee ships that had been intercepted by the British. The DPs had all been sent to Cyprus for internment or back to Germany. The ships were then tied up to the breakwater to rot.

In a rational world every effort is made to provide a ship's passengers with the maximum of safety and comfort. These are not rational times, however; standards were completely different. First, the budget for buying refugee ships was microscopic, dependent on gifts collected abroad in secret. Thus, the only vessels available were World War II remnants abandoned for every use but scrap.

Since refugee ships were only expected to make one short trip— they would either be caught by the British or beached on the shore— the minimum was spent on refitting. To make matters worse for the coming navy, the vessels were literally gutted of their watertight bulkheads to make room for the maximum number of passengers.

Most of these ships were actually caught by the British and were tied up along the quay, free game for British, Arab, and Jewish looting. Everyone stripped anything of value leaving literally worthless hulks. This was the one ray of hope for the navy.

One of Gershon Zak's first moves was to consult with experts from abroad. The first two were shown the refugee ships and it was explained that it was hoped that some could be salvaged for a fleet. Their reaction was to throw up their hands in despair and go home. A navy out of worthless scrap, utter nonsense. Of course they were right.

A third expert suggested a navy based on high-speed motor torpedo boats. He too was right. The only trouble with all the expert advice was that it did not fit the conditions. The only real alternative was to use what was available. Hence, while the British were still occupying Haifa Port, the budding naval organization quietly examined the impounded refugee ships. Several, with a military history, were seen to be possibilities for the navy and work was quietly begun to recondition these.

This work had to be very low key so as not to arouse the curiosity of the British forces. Contractors dressed as stevedores and port personnel were able to work in engine rooms and below decks out of sight.

Three vessels were put into a minimum running condition and were able to set sail from Haifa Port on 23 May. The *Eilat* was an ex-U.S.

Coast Guard icebreaker, and the *Hagana* and *Wedgewood* were ex-Canadian corvettes. They were made to look like ships that had been purchased by foreign owners for commercial use. No one in their right mind would have suspected that these were to be the first ships of the Israeli Navy.

On 21 May these three ships sailed to Tel Aviv, which was their base until the British left Haifa. Had it been available Haifa would have been the natural place to base the navy since there is a large natural bay and the port itself was well developed with a breakwater and piers for cargo handling.

Tel Aviv and Jaffa (adjacent cities now united) have no bay or harbor. Each city had a small lighter port that was used for off-loading cargo from ships anchored off the coast.

The lighters were towed out to the ships where the ship's booms lowered cargo into the waiting lighters. The lighters were then towed back to the ports where the cargo was unloaded. The ports themselves were not large enough to accept a ship, thus the navy vessels had to be anchored offshore where the naval conversion, such as it was, could take place. Later we did have a small base in Jaffa Port, but this was only for emergency repairs of ships anchored offshore.

Gray paint converted the three naval vessels to warships and high numbers painted on their bows, such as K20, K18, and A16 gave the impression of a large fleet. Small field guns on wheels dating back to the late 1800s were tied down on the forward and afterdecks. The whole approach was sheer madness.

The Egyptians had bombarded Caesarea on 2 June and several minor naval encounters had taken place with Israeli ships. However, the one that most characterized the times occurred on 16 June when word was received, from shore observers in the south, that Egyptian ships were sailing north, ostensibly to bombard Tel Aviv.

The *Eilat* set sail at its maximum speed of eight knots to meet the Egyptians, armed with three twenty-millimeter antiaircraft guns and a wooden canon with a sheet metal and canvas turret. From a distance she looked like a formidable opponent, but in reality she had no offensive power whatsoever. Here one can truly gain insight into the people and the times. The Egyptians did not realize that the ship approaching over the horizon had no chance to survive in a naval battle. While on the other hand, the crew of the *Eilat* did not think in these terms. The *Eilat's* crew hadn't a clue on how one fights a naval battle; their ship was a cruel joke. They did have, however, youth; enthusiasm; a strong sense of duty; and most of all, faith.

As the ships converged, the Egyptians commenced firing and made several hits on the *Eilat*. One three-inch shell penetrated the engine room, but did not explode. Weeks later my men removed it. This did not deter the *Eilat;* she kept coming.

The air force then appeared in three waves. In the first, one light plane strafed an Egyptian ship but apparently caused no damage. Awhile later another plane made a similar attack with the same result. Finally, another light plane, a "bomber," appeared. The "bombardier" sat with the bomb in his lap and the pilot practically landed on the deck. The bomb was dropped and caused some small damage, but the plane was shot down, killing both the pilot and bombardier.

Here you see the real secret of Israel's war of liberation. Wonderful young men and women who used every device including their lives to make this dream of a Jewish State a reality. The crew of the *Eilat* did the right thing with their insane unarmed attack: the Egyptians retreated south, and this was their last offensive gesture from the sea. Most of the naval war was won on 4 June off Tel Aviv by a broken-down relic of World War II with a wooden gun. The final coup de grace came later.

# 9
# Getting Acquainted

Now that we are thinking like Israelis in 1948, let's join our innocent abroad. The next morning I was awakened and marveled that here I was in Israel. It was warm and humid with a somewhat musty air. I found my way to the bathroom and while shaving suddenly heard strains of Handel's "Messiah" from some neighbor's phonograph. What could be more appropriate?

Breakfast was another pleasant surprise. A typical Israeli breakfast. Two carts loaded with innumerable goodies were wheeled up to my table. Rolls, jams, cheeses, tomatoes, carrots, peppers, yogurt, an endless array, and again Israeli orange juice. What a way to start a day, much less a new life.

The duty officer of the previous night came to collect me and we were off to headquarters to meet Lova Eliav who was head of administration of the navy. The trip through the city gave me my first real look at Israel. The buildings were all low, two to three stories, and all looked as if they had seen better days. Stone or concrete with stucco was the only building material in evidence and there were blast walls in front of the entrances of most buildings. However, most of these dated from World War II. Some of the buildings showed some rather interesting features such as balconies and arched windows indicating that they had once been elegant. That day, however, the city looked pretty rundown and neglected.

Lova was typical of most naval appointments of the day. He had been in the British Army during the war. Why suddenly promoted to a senior post in the navy? Because he was the best available. In this case, a first-class decision. Lova spoke excellent English and after a few minutes conversation, suggested that we meet with Gershon Zak.

Gershon was quite pleasant, but our conversation was limited by the fact that he spoke no English and my Hebrew was limited to *shalom*. Lova translated and it was agreed that I would go off to inspect the facilities in Haifa and report back the following day.

An aide by the name of Haim Boykis was found, who took very good care of me during the coming days. Haim was typical of a number of young men I was to meet. At the ripe old age of twelve he found life in Germany impossible and in desperation decided to strike out on his own and try to reach Palestine. One should remember that then, as now, Palestine was the only place a Jewish refugee would be welcomed—even at the age of twelve.

The manner of travel was simple; one walked alone or with one other so as not to attract attention. In some cities or towns with sizable Jewish populations, there were hostels, but for the most part this was a lonely trek until one reached a port and transport to Palestine. Then, of course, one had to hurdle the final obstacle, the British blockade.

Haim was a survivor and managed to get to Palestine; he also managed to get me to all the right places in the next few days. We were issued a jeep with a driver, and were on our way. Before leaving for Haifa, however, we returned to the hotel where I had to pick up my things and check out, a procedure that proved to be very strange indeed.

The owner's daughter—about my age—was behind the desk in the lobby and I explained that I was about to leave and wanted to pay. As I took out my wallet she turned pale and grabbed my hand and dragged me into the lavatory.

For a moment I began to wonder if my virtue was in jeopardy. Then she explained, "Today is Saturday—Shabat—and you are not supposed to handle money. Some of the people in the lobby are religious and would be very upset to see you pay, but you can pay me here."

As I payed I couldn't help but wonder about what they might think if they saw me pay her in the lavatory.

David Maimon, one of the navy's captains, hitched a ride with us to his kibbutz, but since David spoke but little English, the conversation was very limited. However, one comment has always stuck with me. The coastal road was now open and we passed long stretches of sand dunes. At one point I asked David if his kibbutz had been sand before they settled the land, and he grunted, "No, swamp."

As was the custom, we stopped at the a roadhouse for our halfway stop and here I saw a scene typical of those days. A number of trucks were parked in the yard, but none of these had a hood over the engine. In fact, later I noticed that most trucks had their hoods removed. These were all prewar relics and in order to keep them in operation the engines needed constant attention. In fact, starting up was a two-man operation, the driver and "Yankel," who was always up on a fender leaning into the engine, while the driver shouted instructions.

It was months before new vehicles began to arrive and it was only after the new ones were on the road that we saw trucks with the engines covered.

Another interesting thing about the trip was that we not only drove through Faradis—Israel's largest Arab village—but we stopped to buy some fruit. Faradis means "paradise" in Arabic.

Despite the activity of the Arab irregulars who had closed the road the night before, Faradis was quiet. During the war I drove through the village many times at all hours of the day and night without any feeling of danger.

Apparently, in the very early stages of the conflict, the town's elders had approached those of the local Jewish settlements and had stated that they had no hostile intent and wanted to live in peace. So that's the way it was.

After Faradis the journey was uneventful, except for a number of bridges over small gulleys that were blown up. At each bridge was a warning sign and one had to turn off the road and drive down into the gulley and up the other side to get back on the road.

We soon reached Haifa and went directly to the port. First, we met the local head of the navy, but instead of one there were actually five different people, all in charge. I think most were happy to see someone relieve them of an unplesant and thoroughly unfamiliar burden. These small headquarters were all remnants of the illegal immigration days when ships were the key means of transport.

From here we went to the port and there I was to be rechristened. The port offices have a short tower from which one can see the entire port and there I met Aaron Shimshoni who was the port commander, well, sort of. Aaron was an American, ex-navy, and had been a port commander somewhere in the Pacific during the war.

As he explained, insofar as foreigners were concerned, particularly U.S. Navy personnel who were part of the U.N. Observer Corps, he was helping the port commander who didn't speak English and had no experience in administering a port. In reality, however, he was the port commander.

At this point he suddenly asked me: "Gershenow isn't really your name, is it?" At which I answered, somewhat taken aback: "Why wouldn't it be my name?"

He replied, "Come here and take a look." Down below us on the quay were two U.S. Navy lieutenants out for a stroll. Aaron then asked me how many lieutenants I knew who spoke four languages. These officers were there as truce observers, but were obviously part of Naval Intelligence. Aaron explained that since we were still legally in the U.S. Naval Reserve, one really ought to have another name.

It was then that trusty Haim said, "You know your name is not really Gershenow in any case." A fine time to tell me. As Haim explained, Gershon was the son of Moses and Gershenow had most probably been Gershonov, meaning from the family of Gershon. The Hebrew equivalent was Gershoni, which is about as common in Israel as Brown or Jones are in America.

So, on the spot I became Haim Gershoni and no one ever knew it had been otherwise. This new name had unexpected advantages, for in the past whenever a stranger wanting to write my name on a form would ask my name I automatically said Gershenow: *G-E-R-S-H-E-N-O-W.* In Israel one merely said Gershoni and this any child can spell.

Aaron brought me up-to-date on who was who and who did what; in addition to the briefing I had a wonderful view of the port. Only one or two ships were in and these furnished a pleasant surprise.

According to maritime custom, a ship entering a foreign port hoists the host country's flag above the flag of the ship's country as a gesture of recognition of the host's sovereignty. There were Israeli flags on every yard arm. It took a bit of getting used to.

Then we began a tour of the workshops. At this point the entire naval shore establishment consisted of but forty men, including the five commanders and their staffs, plus the one or two technical supervisors and workers.

The machine shop was an abandoned workshop of the public works department. The British had, as a matter of policy, closed down public services and had refused to hand over the various services to the new authorities. That which was worth having they took, sold, or destroyed. The machine shop was obviously far below these standards. There was an old lathe, drill, and a shaper, plus two welding machines. Hardly a navy yard, but a start.

The carpentry shop, however, was a gem set up by an ex-manual training teacher. Unfortunately, warships try to avoid the use of wood since it is a fire hazard and splinters from exploading shells can be deadly. However, we did have some small wood patrol boats and for months we broke all the rules concerning using wood aboard the larger ships. When you have no alternatives, it's easy to break the rules.

From there we visited the small craft flotilla. There we found three ex-British Navy patrol crafts that had come to us in a very strange way. Just prior to their leaving Haifa Port—30 June—the British informed the Israeli government that they wished to leave three coastal patrol craft to the new government and would the competent authority make himself known to accept the vessels?

Gershon Zak could not imagine what this was all about, but he met with the British and presented his credentials as head of the navy. The

British then took him on a tour of the three patrol crafts that had been cleaned and polished. As he later put it, he could not believe his eyes. When Ben Gurion heard about the ships, he commented, "This I'll have to see." No one understood why these were turned over to Israel in light of the overall British policy, but such a gift was like manna from heaven.

The boats now had Hebrew names. The *Tirtzah* and the *Dror* were small wooden patrol boats, and the *Portzeme* was a wooden motor launch fitted out with seats as in a bus. Since the country's border, according to the partition plan, was only ten miles at Natanya, from the sea, the specter of the Arabs driving across this narrow neck to the sea must have been a nightmare to the army.

Such a move would have separated the north from the south, and the *Portzeme* was the answer, at least to the question of transportation between the two separated parts of the country if this occurred.

Nothing was operable, which was apparently why they were abandoned. Of course there were no guns or armament, which was par for the course. However, the hulls were in good condition and the engines were repairable.

Then off to see the big ships, and an even more dismal picture. None were operating and no spare parts were available. Living conditions were largely nonexistent. Men slept on the steel decks and ate cold food since the ships had no bunks or galley ranges. Radar and proper radios were unavailable although some small army field radios had been scrounged. These led to another surprise. For some reason, most of the radio operators were girls. Ships also carried nurses. In those days there was complete sexual equality and women fought alongside men in combat units.

The armaments were virtually useless. The two corvettes each had a French seventy-five millimeter field gun dating from World War I roughly bolted to the forward decks, and a forty-millimeter mountain gun with a barrel three feet long aft. These reputedly dated from the Napoleonic wars. This was it.

To fully understand the utterly deplorable state of the navy, one must realize that naval vessels are subdivided by bulkheads and decks so that in case of damage the flooding will be controlled and the ship will stay afloat. Such subdivisions had long since been cut away to make room for immigrants.

Guns on a naval vessel are part of a highly technical integrated system. Since everything on water is moving, we have a rolling ship moving in a given direction at a given speed firing at another ship that is at an unknown distance and also moving in its own direction and speed. Thus to hit the enemy there must be a highly complex integrated system having range finders, computers, ammunition handling systems, communications, and highly trained crews all working together.

We had none of these and bolting antiques to the decks was only a gesture to improve morale and impress the enemy. As Jimmy Durante used to say, "Dems de conditions what prevailed."

# 10
# The Big Parade

After reviewing the fleet it was pretty late, so we called it a day and checked into the Zion Hotel. After dinner we found Vic and Judy's phone number and fortunately they were home and extended a very hearty welcome and invitation to drop over. Haim and our driver dropped me at the Avrunins and were to call for me in a couple of hours.

We had lots of catching up to do. Vic was now transportation officer for the northern part of the country. His workshops were already busy rehabilitating the war surplus vehicles he had purchased and he had a number of bases and units under his command, all madly trying to put the army's transport into some sort of fighting shape.

The conversation got around to the navy and they were most curious as to what I had found and how I felt about the situation. Finally, Vic said: "OK Hal, what are you going to do now?" Since seeing the ships and facilities during the day, things had begun to crystallize in my mind and I explained how I thought the new navy yard should be organized as well as the program for the immediate future. I had even drawn up an organization chart based on the facilities and people I had met. As per my instructions from Gershon Zak, I planned to report back the next day with these recommendations.

Then came the best advice I have ever received. "Hal, that's not enough. You've got to take charge. No one knows what to do about the navy yard. You've got to make it clear that you've come to do the job and take over. You'll see that Gershon will be pleased to get some of these problems off his head onto yours."

About this time Haim showed up with the jeep. On leaving, Vic and Judy insisted that on my return to Haifa, I stay with them. As they put it, that's the way things are done here and we won't have it any other way.

By this time my mind was really in a turmoil, but Haim had brought along a little surprise for the road. The jeep had no brakes. We were at the top of Mount Carmel. How does one go down a mountain without brakes? "Oh, it's not so difficult," explained the driver. "I'll put it into four-wheel drive on the steep parts. Don't worry; it will be *beseder.*" My second Hebrew word—meaning "OK." Well, it was beseder, but I must have lost a few pounds on the way down to the hotel.

The next morning the trip back to Haifa was uneventful and left me with plenty of time to mull over Vic's advice. The whole idea of simply taking over seemed completely outrageous, for I had been a lieutenant not an admiral. I was a foreigner, far from my own turf; how could I charge in and tell them that since Gershoni was here, it will all be beseder?

Actually, Gershon Zak made the whole business very easy. He wanted a detailed account of what I'd seen and what I recommended. When I showed him my organization chart of the proposed navy yard he asked: "Where do you see yourself?" With much more outward confidence than I felt, I pointed to the top position of officer in charge. He nodded and said, "Go ahead." Thus a few minutes later I received a one-line set of orders stating that Gershoni was in charge of the navy yard.

Those with a military background have probably noted that I had not been inducted into the Israeli Navy and despite this minor oddity I had just been appointed to a very senior position. This is a perfect example of why one must understand the times in order to understand specific events. Actually, at that time there were no formalities for inducting new recruits. Moreover, Gershon simply did not have any other alternatives.

Some Israelis had served in the Jewish Brigade during the war so some officers and trained men were available for the new Israeli Army. Arms and equipment had been hidden from the British during the Mandate and now additional equipment had begun to arrive from overseas. The navy, however, had no such base in trained men or equipment and literally had been able to openly operate for only three weeks. Thus it is not so strange that Gershon Zak grasped the only straw available.

Trusty Haim arranged for a pocket-sized Rennault to be assigned to me and informed me that we were not off to Haifa. That afternoon we were going to a parade.

Military parades in Israel are hardly for the public's enjoyment, although some have been quite spectacular. Usually these are held to display Israel's military capability to our hostile neighbors in order to provide some serious food for thought.

In July 1948, however, the problem had an odd twist. There was a rising tide of apprehension abroad that Israel could not survive in the face of the overwhelming size of the surrounding enemies. Some news had more or less filtered out of Israeli victories and the world had heard of the Haganah, but there was little real evidence of an army that could indeed prevent another Holocaust. Hence, the twenty-seventh of June, the anniversary of Theodore Herzl's birth, was called Nation Day. Moreover, it was to be celebrated with Israel's first military parade. The diplomatic corps and foreign press were all invited and it was to be a gala occasion.

Since we had some time before the parade, I thought it a good idea to buy some proper Israeli clothes. It was hot and everyone seemed to be wearing shorts and knee socks, which seemed like just the thing for me. Haim took me to the proper shops nearby and I got my first taste of being a Jew in Israel. In every shop he told the proprietor that, "This Jew is looking for _____"

Where I had grown up we did not hide the fact that we were Jews, but we didn't advertise it either. Moreover, if someone referred to you on the street as a Jew, it was usually not in a complimentary sense. However, Haim was using the expression as, "this fellow," because everyone was a Jew. As he was speaking I suddenly realized that there in Tel Aviv everyone was Jewish. It was a strange new sensation to suddenly be like everyone else. Here a dirty Jew was someone who needed a bath. It took awhile to become acclimatized.

Most of the army's heavy equipment had been freshly painted and brought to Tel Aviv for the event. Uniforms for the troops presented an awkward problem for the organizers in that no two members of any unit had the same uniform. It would be some time before Vic's purchases in the United States began to arrive.

All sorts of khaki shirts and trousers appeared, all remnants of World War II. The worst problem, however, was with the hats and helmets. German, British, American, you name it we had them. The army simply looked like rabble. A problem solved with typical Israeli ingenuity.

On the spot it was decided what each unit was to wear and soldiers began a mass strip tease as they exchanged bits and pieces of their uniforms. Finally, every soldier wore the uniform of his particular unit. Of course each unit had its own distinctive uniform. The public only saw the final result.

The parade itself served its purpose; an army was displayed together with an assortment of heavy equipment all of which implied that Israel could defend herself. Much of the equipment was obviously home-made; captured equipment was also proudly displayed.

One minor incident that particularly pleased me was that as one typical infantry unit passed, the sergeant called out the cadence in very southern U.S. English.

After the parade we finally headed for Haifa, where in the succeeding days I learned that despite our victories and parade, how badly prepared we were to fight established armed forces.

# 11
# Getting Organized

The very first day it was obvious that our prime concern was the establishment of some sort of organization, and that morning five key appointments were made. The first was Lauterbach-Lotar—who was an electrical engineer, an ex-lieutenant in the British Navy and, most important, fluent in English and Hebrew. Many people spoke Hebrew and English, but fluency in written Hebrew was not quite so common.

Unfortunately, my Hebrew vocabulary was limited to about three words, but I soon learned *maspenah*, which means "shipyard." The most useful word of my vocabulary was *beseder*, roughly meaning "OK." It's amazing how much you can accomplish with one such word (particularly if your counterpart speaks English).

In an American navy yard the real manager was a civilian with the title of chief clerk. The admiral was legally the boss, but he usually served in such a post for only two years, whereas the continuity of power was with the chief clerk. I thought Lauterbach would be thrilled as I described the post, but to my utter amazement he declared, "Sir, I am an engineer and you can court-martial me, but I will not be a clerk."

To gain time while recovering from the shock, I looked over my list of billets—all four of them—and finally said, "Well, the only other appropriate job would be administration officer, "how would you like that?" This was much more acceptable so after changing the title on my list from chief clerk to administration officer, we were off and running.

Lauterbach's (now: Lotar) first tasks were to find us an office, suitable buildings in the port for workshops, and lay out some sort of work order procedure.

Steuer (now: Haim Sarton) was also an electrical engineer, an ex-lieutenant in the British Navy, with extensive experience in ship repairs. He became our electrical repair officer. He knew exactly what to do—find some equipment, especially a test stand; locate some assistants; and start putting the fleet's electrical equipment in order.

Joe Novick was a natural for his job as machinery repair officer. He had years of experience repairing all sorts of heavy equipment, and there was no need to tell him what to do. Five minutes later he was busy resurrecting our ancient machine shop.

Yaacov Krauss had a background in precision instrument repairs, so he became head of the instrument shop. The carpentry was already in good hands and this left me with only one more appointment for the day, Schneider (now: Shlomo Dovrat). He had worked for the electric company as an engineer and he seemed to know his way around the marketplace so he became a special assistant with the prime task of locating equipment.

On the spot—all of these meetings were held standing since we had no office—I gave Schneider a list of equipment including seven welding machines. He looked at me in amazement because people in Israel did not think in such quantities. He then politely suggested that perhaps one welding machine and perhaps one or two of the other items might be better for a start.

This brought on a short speech that I was to use quite often. "We are building the country's navy and this cannot be done as one would start a small workshop." It took him a while to get used to these new terms of reference, but he did a fine job.

We had no candidate for hull repair officer so I decided to look after this until we could find someone suitable. Strangely enough, everyone accepted the new regime and went to work. It was as if they were grateful that some sort of organization was beginning to appear and they could all get on with the job.

Literally, within days, the new organization began to take hold. Ships' personnel knew where to go with their repair problems, every work request was recorded, and a proper expert checked the job and recommended the proper solution. Finally, every request was ultimately completed. At the beginning our facilities were very limited so subcontractors were employed, but with time we were able to build a facility that could take over all of the repairs for the navy.

Workers for the maspenah were another basic problem, but here we had an enormous pool of labor from which to pick. Over ten thousand displaced persons were arriving each month. None of the great powers had been able to accept even a tiny portion, but we received them all with open arms.

These were Jews from all walks of life; they had first been in concentration camps and then at the end of the war had languished in DP camps, for no country would accept them. Now they were flooding into Israel. To me, that's what it was all about.

Anyone who had doubts about the State of Israel had only to witness the arrival of one of these ships to straighten out their thinking. I was to witness this scene several times each week, and even today, after forty years, the memory brings a lump to my throat. The ships were battered old tubs, no longer useful for any other purpose. As they approached the quay the newcomers lined the rails in tatters, stooped, haggard, faces carrying the imprint of their years in concentration camps. Not a smile, they scarcely moved. However, as the ship approached a miracle occurred. They straightened up and assumed a new dignity as they proudly sang "Hatikvah" ("The Hope"—Israel's national anthem).

This was not just an arrival at another stop along the way. After undergoing unbelievable brutality at the hands of the Nazis, they had waited in camps for two years. No one wanted them and aside from an occasional "What a pity," the Gentile world was prepared to let them rot where they were. Now, they were home.

Some of these newcomers were absorbed into the community within hours. Every army unit had a representative at the reception center and we were certainly no exception. As soon as some useful talent appeared, somebody grabbed him to fill a vacant billet.

The *Portzeme*, one of our inherited motor launches, was a perfect example. She had sophisticated high-performance gasoline engines and we had no one who knew how to care for such equipment. Then one day our man at the reception center struck gold. A real expert appeared, but there was one small problem. He only spoke Hungarian. What to do? The obvious. We found a youngster who spoke Hebrew and Hungarian and made him the expert's assistant.

This was a problem to plague us for many years. Everyone spoke several languages, but not always the same ones. Many people did speak Hebrew, but could not read and write it. Hence, superimposed on all one's other problems was the nagging problem of communicating.

In the beginning English was the language of the air force and the navy. The infantry spoke Hebrew and it was said that some artillery units spoke Russian. Apparently, the Russians were expert artillerymen and at the end of the war some of the Russian Jews from these units were able to slip away and find their way to Israel.

On one of these very early days I was standing on the deck of a seagoing tug we were resurrecting from the fleet of dead refugee ships, when a man approached me and in perfect English said: "Sir, can you tell me what do do?" This was a bit strange, for no one called me sir. It's just not the Israeli way. Hal, perhaps, or even hey you, but certainly not sir.

I had no idea who he was or what he wanted. So I asked what was the problem and he replied, "Sir, I arrived in this country yesterday and everything I have in the world is on my back. I'm an expert boilermaker and am working on the ship's boiler, but look!" With that he raised his foot and I saw what was apparently a normal shoe, but one without a sole. He continued, "I can't work on a hot boiler in my bare feet."

This really touched a very sensitive nerve, for none of my men had uniforms or proper clothing. For some reason, this man without shoes reminded me of Washington crossing the Delaware with men whose feet were wrapped in bloody rags.

Fortunately, some of Vic's uniforms had just arrived, and after throwing a fit at headquarters, my men were each issued a second-hand shirt, a second-hand pair of trousers, and a used pair of army boots. The luxury of it all.

The whole concept of men in uniforms with specified ranks was at this time completely nonexistent in the entire military establishment. Moreover, no one had a uniform or insignia; thus one could not be sure who was who. In some cases, men involved with our work were not even in the navy and one had no way of knowing.

My uniform was usually khaki shorts, knee socks, and an American sport shirt. One of my favorites was a T-shirt having red, white, and blue, stripes, each four inches wide. It must have looked strange to Haifaites, for one day a stranger stopped me on the street and announced that it was a long time to Purim. (This is a festival when children dress up in costumes, like Halloween in the United States.)

It took awhile to get used to the numbers tattooed on the arms of so many people, but we were getting used to each other. One new arrival described the luxury of being in a place where people did not stare. No, we didn't stare, but I must confess that even today it gives me a bit of a shock to see a forearm with a number.

During this period another type of personnel began to appear—volunteers from abroad—the Machal (volunteers from abroad). Paul Shulman, an Annapolis graduate, lieutenant in the U.S. Navy, and veteran of World War II, was our first chief of staff. He had been in the Israeli Navy from the very beginning but since he was in the United States when I had arrived, I wasn't to meet him until some time later.

One day, while aboard the *Portzeme*, one of the sailors struck up a conversation in very British English. It turned out that David De-Lange had been a lieutenant in the British Navy during the war and had also been a flotilla leader of motor launches such as the *Portzeme*.

He, too, had felt the need to be a part of Israel's birth and had left his wife and son behind and come to volunteer. The route had to be via a DP camp in Marseilles and he arrived as a DP. Apparently no one at the recruiting center had appreciated his backgorund, for he was assigned to the ship as a simple sailor. However, this oversight was quickly remedied. David was really a fine addition to the navy and ultimately rose to be chief of naval operations.

Allan Burke was another British volunteer who came on his own to join the navy. Allan had been a lieutenant commander in the British Navy, captain of a frigate, and truly an experienced naval officer with a great deal of combat experience. He later became flotilla commander of the large ships.

Over two thousand volunteers came from abroad to volunteer in the various services of Israel's armed forces. By and large these were secular Jews who were motivated by national rather than religious motives. There were experienced experts in almost every field who had served in the Allied armies of World War II.

Well, our navy, such as it was, began to function. Each day brought strange new problems, but we did begin to do our job. Unfortunately, we had a long long way to go.

# 12
# Teething

Within a day after the initial appointments of our maspenah staff, things began to move. First, Lauterbach found us a temporary office near the port and started negotiations for the number five shed of the port. This was a huge warehouse near the pier where the navy ships were tied up. However, progress on other fronts was burdened with all sorts of unanticipated teething problems.

My instructions to all the department heads were to let me know immediately if they had a problem that required my help; they did not disappoint me. On the spot, Steuer explained that we had to have a test bench for checking motors, but this would have to be made to order. This was a straightforward issue requiring only a set of specifications and quotations from local electrical workshops. I say workshops here, for there were no local industrial plants; such work was done in small workshops employing but a few workers.

Joe Novick approached me the next day with a much more complex problem. Could he have one hundred pounds (about $250) to buy some micrometers and other measuring instruments? One can see that we really were starting from the very beginning since he had nothing of this sort. The money here was not the issue. The real question was: "What measuring system—English or metric?"

The country had been largely settled by Europeans, hence most people thought in metric units. However, much of our equipment, such as the ships and their engines, were from the United States, Canada, or England, which meant English units. Moreover, importers in those days took what they could get. One day it would be a ten-pound plate from the United States. This weighed ten pounds a square foot and is ¼ inches thick. The next time he might find a 6-millimeter plate from France and this is close to ¼ inches, but not exactly the same.

Thus we simply had to be able to deal in both systems, which meant not only duplicate measuring instruments, but a whole range of duplicate tools such as metric and English wrenches. The most important thing was that everyone had to think in both systems as a matter of routine.

A day or so later the radio experts came to me with the question: "Where do we put the radios?" This normally would be a silly question since the radios go in the radio shack, where else? In our situation the ships had been stripped and altered so often that we found the radio shacks usually being used for other purposes. In one case a likely spot was suggested, which I found to be the wardroom pantry.

When I explained that the wardroom—officers' mess—had to have a pantry in order to serve hot food, it was explained to me that the Israeli Navy was socialist and officers ate with the men in the crew's mess. This sounded quite commendable, but there were repercussions that had not been anticipated.

This problem came to a head in just a few days when one of the captains insisted that we construct more officers' cabins on his ship. He had no place for his officers to sleep. At first, I had visions of the South American navy ships of World War II with more officers than men, but we were equipping ships with the same complement as the Americans. On checking one of the ships, all became clear.

They had taken the original officers' cabins and instead of putting two to a cabin, each cabin was fitted for one and contained a large desk. Why the desk? Because there was no place for the officers to do their paperwork. Actually the wardroom is for such work on a small ship, and the wardrooms had been taken from the officers in the name of democracy. Fortunately, we decided that the U.S. approach had been successful and then was not the time to try social experiments. So, the ships went back to the way they were originally designed.

It should be noted that although these ships had all been equipped with radar during World War II, radar was entirely outside our expectations. Such equipment was simply unavailable. The first radar in the navy was put together from miscellaneous junk by a British volunteer—Harvey Miller—who was a physicist and had been a lieutenant in the British Navy. This first unit was installed at Navy Headquarters on top of Mount Carmel. The ships did not receive radar until long after the war.

Our two main preoccupations were engines and guns or really, the lack of these. There were no spare parts and most of the time nothing could move. In those early times Avram Zaki, the operations officer, would approach me with a request for anything that could sail that night. When I'd explain that I had nothing for him, he'd bargain. It's only for eight hours." Then I'd counter with, "We don't even have a four-hour ship."

On one such day Joe Novick reported that the nearest he had to an eight-hour ship was one of the British motor launches, but he needed a starter, a piston, and a connecting rod for the engine and there simply was no source of supply.

However, about an hour later he came back to me and said that he needed some money in cash. He explained the following: when the British were in Palestine they had a number of launches similar to ours and when they left they moved anything worthwhile to Cyprus including their spare parts. Apparently these had been dumped someplace out of the way and were more or less forgotten. However, not by everyone.

The Steele Brothers Importing Company had moved their headquarters to Cyprus when the British left despite their extensive interests in Palestine. To keep in touch with Israel they had a motor launch, similar to ours, which made the trip to Cyprus several times a week.

Apparently, one of the crew was quite resourceful at scrounging and knew more or less the sort of things we needed, so that day he had offered Joe a starter, connecting rod, and piston for one hundred pounds—less than cost price. Needless to say, Avram Zaki had his eight-hour boat.

Such miracles were by no means unique and apparently happened in all the units to the point that the expression, "If you don't believe in miracles, you're not a realist," became quite common. Unfortunately, people came to rely on such miracles, but I don't recall any disappointments.

Another of Joe's victories in the machine shop made us aware of a whole new series of problems: transport and training of crews. The fan engine on one of the corvettes was completely worn out. This was an engine that drove the blower supplying air for combustion in the boiler. Joe's crew rebuilt the engine with great care and devotion and when it was finished he very proudly informed me that it was just like new. There was one small problem, however. He couldn't get a truck to move it from the old public works shop outside the port to the ship.

I glibly said, "No problem, hire a truck." Whereupon he explained that there were no trucks for hire. It seems that the army was in the midst of a major operation and since the army did not have sufficient transport they simply requisitioned everything on wheels. Ultimately, the fan engine went to the port on a wagon pulled by a horse.

In this same vein there was a story told about how Yael Dayan asked her daddy one day whether "the attack" would take place that day. He was apparently amazed at her knowledge of supposedly secret plans and asked how she knew about such things. She replied, "Oh, Daddy, all the kids know that when there are no buses it's because you took them all to move soldiers and there is going to be an attack someplace."

Our problems with the fan engine did not end with its delivery to the ship. The ship sailed that afternoon and returned the next day with the engine smashed and out of action again.

Apparently the crew was green as grass and after several hours the engine began to knock. Experienced engineers would have recognized this as normal after an overhaul and would have stopped the engine, tightened the bearings, and continued the operation. This crew, however, did not realize what was happening and were afraid to stop the engine. So it smashed itself to pieces. It took years until the training problem was in hand.

Guns were a much more complex problem, for these were not readily available. One day, however, word got to us that some proper three-inch and four-inch naval guns were on the way. Since these were not the sort of things that could be simply bolted to the decks, I pressed our headquarters to get us some plans of the guns so we could design proper foundations and platforms for the ships. In due course we did get the plans and our very new design department began to make the necessary calculations and drawings. Fortunately, we did make this start, for several weeks later, all hell broke loose and the guns had to be mounted literally in three days.

Usually, however, our planning was a much more rudimentary process. Twenty-mm guns are most important to naval vessels since they are used against both aircraft and surface targets. However, as with most equipment, we had no such goodies.

Our first twenty-millimeter gun was not a great success since it had been used by some European army in the field. It had three little legs and the gunner sat on a small seat and aimed the gun by turning two little handles. This may well have been acceptable in the field artillery, but on a ship one would have to spin the little wheels like mad to track a plane.

This gun was delivered in the very first days when there simply was no time to sit down and work out such problems of how to mount a twenty-millimeter field gun on a ship. As we considered the problem, someone's glance fell on an abandoned searchlight base and he said, "If we turn that thing upside down we can weld it to the deck and the gun can be welded to the top." That was it, and just like in a television movie, the job was done within an hour.

This gun was actually wasted on a ship and prompted a number of urgent meetings on the proper type of twenty-millimeter guns for the ships. A week or so later I was informed by a breathless messenger that we had actually received two genuine twenty-millimeter naval guns.

These two were for the whole navy when thirty would have more appropriate, but it sounded too good to be true.

When I arrived at the machine shop there they were, but without the mounts. It seems that the mounts had been pinched by a commando unit so that jeeps could be fitted with similar guns. There was no time for protests, so on the spot a mount was designed on the back of an envelope.

American mounts have a device for raising and lowering the gun so the gunner could sight higher or lower as the need arose without having to bend or stoop. Such refinements were out of our league at the time. The new Israeli mounts consisted of a piece of oil well casing with an old ball bearing and a simple clevis support for the gun. Our gunners had to stoop, but that was a price we were prepared to pay.

Israelis were quite used to making do. Abroad, if some part or assembly was worn you chucked it out and installed a new one. In Palestine, and now Israel, such items were carefully taken apart and repaired, for new ones were never available. This sort of thing was happening in all our shops. One day Krauss met me on the street and complained that since his appointment as head of the instrument repair shop that, although we met each day in my office, I hadn't been to see his shop. The reason was of course lack of time.

On the spot I said, "Lets go," since heaven only knew when there would be a better time. To my great surprise he had set up a beautiful instrument shop where his men were busy reconditioning binoculars, compasses, and even a sextant taken from a local museum.

A short time later he was in the office and overheard Izzie, our office manager, complain that we still had no Hebrew typewriter and all letters had to be handwritten. Krauss immediately offered to convert an English machine to Hebrew, if we could get him the English typewriter.

At first glance this sounded easy, in that one need only replace the keys with readily available Hebrew characters. The real problem, however, is that Hebrew is written from right to left, thus the carriage of an English machine must be made to move backward. This didn't phase Krauss; he knew exactly what had to be done. A used English machine was found and a short time later the office was in business with a Hebrew typewriter with handmade parts.

Another similar case occurred in the machine shop where one day I saw the unbelievable sight of a man making a gear with hand tools. This was too much to believe so I called over Joe and insisted that there must be a milling machine in Haifa that could make the gear.

Joe's answer was, "There are only five milling machines in the entire Haifa area and each is booked for weeks. This part is needed tonight and the toolmaker with golden hands is our only chance." The part was delivered on time.

In America the obvious solution would be to go out and buy a milling machine, but such a solution was not within our terms of reference. First of all, industrial development of the country was in its infancy, which in turn, meant that such equipment was not stocked by suppliers. Actually, Schneider finally solved the problem by buying a whole machine shop just to get their milling machine.

With all of these problems we were in operation and slowly the maspenah and the navy were taking shape. In a sense, life on the home front was following a similar pattern.

# 13
# The Calm before the Storm

During the next few weeks we all began to settle down to our respective jobs and slowly a certain amount of order began to appear. In a sense, we entered a period of the calm before the storm. My life, however, involved more than just engines and guns, and I found that all sorts of interesting things were happening outside the navy.

The United Nations was certainly one of the major irritants of the time, for despite the fact that we were created by the United Nations, they seemed to be dedicated to our annihilation. We were invaded by seven member states but no one, not the United Nations or the superpowers would lift a finger to help us. Then to make matters worse, they refused to sell us arms and imposed an arms embargo.

The United Nations assumed the role of inspector to prevent what arms we could obtain from reaching Israel. Obviously, one Holocaust was enough; we had to find ways of helping ourselves. Some of these had humorous overtones.

One day an ex-German landing craft came into port with a load of eggs. Eggs? Somehow or other this smelled of skulduggery. So the United Nations inspectors eagerly opened every one of the huge cases only to learn that these contained eggs as specified in the manifest.

It did seem odd to me that the overzealous inspectors concentrated on the cargo and ignored the landing craft that became a part of the navy.

Usually I got to the port early in the morning, long before the United Nations personnel and one day there were hundreds of half tracks brazenly lined up along the quay. Since tracked vehicles were on the forbidden list, I raced to a phone to call Vic since he was in charge of transport for the north. His laconic comment was, "It's OK Hal; I'll tell you all about it tonight."

That evening Vic announced that the half tracks were being transshipped to Turkey—an unheard-of procedure in those days. These were to be shipped out that night on the *Richard Borchard*, a British ship owned by a very sympathetic Jewish family. The interesting thing, however, was the Turkish firm's name on the manifest. The half tracks were consigned to "Kishmir Ltd, Istanbul" (for the non-linguist, Kishmir is the first word of a very useful Yiddish expression; *Kishmir im tochas,* or "Kiss my ass.").

Sure enough, the next morning both the *Richard Borchard* and the half tracks were gone.

One of the many unexpected problems that surfaced with the import of vehicles was the fact that Israel had no drivers. Why? Very simple, very few people owned private cars; hence kids did not learn to drive as in the United States.

Many units found the thrill of at last receiving a truck, jeep, or half track turn into a nightmare due to the fact that no one knew how to drive it. This in turn led to a massive effort to train drivers. For the next year, we saw long convoys of trucks with learner drivers.

It was about this time that my diet of quick snacks standing at the various lunch counters began to take its toll. As most newcomers to the Middle East at that time, my stomach was having great difficulty in coping with the diet and local intestinal wild life. I decided that henceforward lunch was going to be a quiet half hour in a respectable restaurant where no one could see me from the street.

This last qualification was most important, for a great deal of business was done on the street. If someone with a problem saw me, we often had a meeting on the street that could lead to an urgent visit to a ship or workshop. Hence I wanted to disappear during lunch.

The Eden Café was just the place. The restaurant was L shaped and I noted that if I sat at the bottom of the L no one could see me from the street, insuring a quiet meal.

The waiter was an elderly German and when he came to take my order I said, "I'm sick and if I get any sicker I'm going to hold you personally responsible. Please bring me anything you know is OK." He laughed and said, "You can trust me." His name was Max and this was the beginning of a very friendly relationship. Each day I would sit down and Max would simply put a meal before me. Whatever he brought I ate.

The first day he put a liter bottle of orange juice on the table and I protested saying that in my condition this did not seem very appropriate. Max merely replied, "Drink it; it's good for you." He seemed like a surrogate Jewish mother. From that day on I began to feel better.

One day as I sat down I noticed that the usual assortment of U.N. observers were all enjoying steak so I read my paper anticipating the same. However, Max suddenly put an omelet in front of me. I called him back and asked how come they had steak and I had eggs. He bent over and whispered in my ear, "For them it's good enough. You're going to have an omelet." I never questioned him again.

Life at the Avrunins was very congenial, but this was the first time I had been separated from Marilyn and David. So, despite the heavy work load and my pleasant surroundings, it was somewhat lonely. Every night I would write home telling about the country, and despite the fact that the British had closed down the postal service before they left, the Israeli government had started up the mails again, so Marilyn and I were able to keep in touch.

Later she would remark that I had written everything about the country except how beautiful it was. Such was the mind of a young engineer. Looking back, our views of conditions were a strange anomaly.

We certainly knew that Israel was not at peace for each day during these months of 1948 we saw headlines such as:

17 September     Hour of War Rages in Jerusalem

6 October        Egyptian Army Breaks Lull in Jerusalem

10 October       Egyptians Throw Planes & Guns into Negev Fray

Furthermore, those in positions of responsibility knew that our army was certainly not up to the standards that we would have wished. Each day we saw quotations from the Arab media stating that "We will throw them into the sea," and we truly believed that this is exactly what they would do if given the chance.

On the other hand, we also saw encouraging headlines in our papers such as:

6 August         16 Settlements in 6 Weeks

10 August        10,000 Will Come Every Month

15 September     Fastest Growing State in World

Moreover, our day-to-day living had a certain stability and certainly those in Haifa and Tel Aviv, the areas with which I was familiar, viewed the situation as quite normal. We had complete confidence that we would not be overrun by the enemy and that peace was around the corner.

Hence, after getting the views of my colleagues and friends I wrote to Marilyn to have the furniture packed and arrangements would be made for her and Davy to come to Israel. This was certainly not an extraordinary decision within our terms of reference. Paul Shulman's wife Rose was already in Israel. David Delange and Alan Burke were also making such arrangements.

In America, however, this decision was viewed perhaps a bit more rationally. When my father-in-law, a very calm sort of man, saw my cable, he greeted Marilyn with: "You're going to take your child into the midst of a war?"

They also read headlines about the fighting, but as is usual with newspaper reporting only the "bang" is newsworthy. They saw only the dark side and my decision must have seemed completely mad.

However, in a relatively short time the family got used to the idea and the necessary arrangements were made. Then toward the end of September I received that all-important cable. They were on the way.

Haifa Airport was still the one and only civilian airport in operation and I was there to greet my family on their arrival. Their plane was a very strange little one and when the door opened, out popped little David and Marilyn dressed in the height of New York fashion. Despite my frontier attire Marilyn recognized me, but it did take Davy a few days to get used to having a father.

The Shulmans were staying in a lovely new hotel, the Ben Yehuda, on Mount Carmel. It was small by U.S. standards, but very homey and just right for our first few weeks. The Ben Yehuda became a navy machal—volunteers from abroad—center in Haifa. The navy and the local community made the new families most welcome. Most of our new friends spoke excellent English and there was a small Anglo Saxon-English speaking-community that very quickly absorbed us all into their midst.

Davy's vocabulary was that of a young man fifteen months old. His key word was *Hi!* and unfortunately he came to use it under rather strange circumstances. The second night after their arrival we had an air raid alarm. Haifa was blacked out when the alarm sounded and all the guests of the hotel were asked to come to the lobby that was ostensibly the safest place. We all managed to get settled comfortably in the dark through which we all heard a little voice saying, "Hi! Hi! Hi!"

By the end of August we were beginning to reach the point where ships, particularly the two corvettes, could go to sea when circumstances demanded. This certainly did not mean that they were in perfect working order. It was a long time before there were bunks for the crew and men did not have to sleep on the steel decks. Galley ranges were also late in coming so only cold food was available, but despite the difficulties, the navy functioned.

One branch of the navy that had been functioning even before ships were available were the "Sea Commandos," as they were called in Hebrew. These were youngsters trained in all sorts of sabotage to hit the enemies in the only way we could at the time. When it was learned that the Egyptians were about to send a shipment of arms from Italy to Egypt, the ship mysteriously blew up and sank in an Italian harbor.

This is perhaps an excellent example of our anger at the United Nations. The Egyptians and other Arab countries were able to more or less openly buy arms and send them to their home ports, for the United Nations made no effort to blockade them or enforce the embargo. The United Nations only seemed to enforce the embargo in Haifa.

Later, the cargo from the sunken ship was raised and loaded on another small Italian freighter. Then, toward the end of August, it set sail again for Egypt. Shortly after sailing, the freighter was hailed by a small fishing vessel and two Italian naval officers boarded to guide them to a rendezvous with the Egyptian fleet.

Sure enough, near Crete they met the fleet that curiously enough, consisted of the *Hagana* and the *Wedgewood*. Another oddity was that the two Italian officers were named David Ben Horin and Oved Sadeyh—pure Hebrew names.

As one of the Israeli crew members later put it, they played pirates just like the British when they captured refugee ships on the open sea.

The arms consisting of eight thousand rifles and eight million rounds of ammunition were transferred to the corvettes, which together with the Italian crew, were brought to Haifa. At a party one evening celebrating the successful outcome of the operation, one thing impressed me more than anything about the operation. The two young men who played the key roles, were short, slightly built, unobtrusive, modest young men. The last choice of any Hollywood director for such parts. Perhaps this was why they were successful.

# 14
# Arming the Navy

It seemed like we needed everything and had to make do with all sorts of very inadequate expedients. On the other hand, the truce observers came from countries with an abundance of every conceivable type of equipment. One morning an American navy supply ship came into port to discharge cargo for the United Nations, and I couldn't help but stand there green with envy.

I was dressed in my uniform of shorts and striped T-shirt, and watched with my tongue hanging out. They had everything. There were more guns aboard this one ship than we had in our whole navy. The sailors had proper clothing and what was more important, they all knew what they were doing.

The bosun directing the unloading was on the main deck directly above me with his potbelly bulging over his trousers quietly directing the operation in a manner that reeked with authority and experience. I would have given my right arm for someone like that.

I stood there wallowing in self-pity, belaboring the fact that they at peace had everything, while we at war had nothing, when the officer of the deck approached the rails suddenly I realized that it was "Chips" Moorman who had been my junior division officer aboard the U.S.S. *Altair* during the war.

Even if he had noticed me he couldn't have recognized me due to my odd getup, but I slipped back into the shadows wondering what to do. We had been good friends and it would have been pleasant to say hello. Perhaps I could scrounge something, but what? No, any contact would be looking for trouble, so I sadly slipped away back to the reality of Israel 1948.

Reality was ferreting about the scrap and rubble so abundant after the British left to hunt for bits and pieces that might be useful. About that same time Schneider came to see me and suggested that while scrounging in the port he had come across something that he thought I ought to see.

Scrounging in the various junk heaps and abandoned supplies and equipment from the British was an activity that kept a lot of us very busy. Much of our parts and supplies came from this activity.

One of the ways the British attempted to deprive us of vehicles not worth taking along with them was to push these over cliffs along the top of Mount Carmel into the wadis and set fire to them. For months after they left there were winches along these roads pulling up useful bits and pieces that crews down below were able to salvage. There was even a story about how a tank attack was halted due to the breakdown of one of the armored cars, and how a special team rushed back to the wadi to find the necessary part so the attack could continue.

In this particular case, however, the find was in the port itself. Schneider took me to an out-of-the-way corner where a huge case was stored. The boys had pried open the back and there were two very elegant contra propellers protruding from the transom of what had to be a very special speed boat. These were two propellers on the same shaft and turned in opposite directions. We couldn't see much more than this, but from the propellers it was obvious that this was some sort of very high-performance speedboat.

Since I could not think of any use we would have for such a boat we reluctantly had the boys nail the case shut. Actually I was to see this same boat in the very near future. On the way back to the office, Schneider pointed out some very impressive wooden guns and canvas turrets that had been mounted on the *Eilat* during her battle with the Egyptians.

One afternoon the following week at about five, Yossie Hamburger met me on the street and said he wanted to show me something. We walked a few steps down Kingsway and he suddenly said maybe we should go out to eat something first. So we stopped at Kingsbar for a bite and then set off in Yossie's car.

It was soon dark and I had no idea where we were going or if we would arrive, for Yossie drove like a madman. We were somewhere in the mountains and literally screeching around hairpin turns on two wheels. Fortunately, the ordeal did not continue very long and we descended into the city of Tiberias on the Sea of Galilee. We finally arrived at one of the seaside hotels and then the mystery began to unravel.

One of our agents abroad while looking for armament for our ships found an ideal answer for a pauper's navy. Explosive motorboats. During the war the Italians had developed small high-speed motorboats armed with a two hundred and fifty-kilogram charge of TNT. The driver aimed the boat at the ship to be sunk and about one hundred yards before crashing into the ship he pulled a lever that dumped him from the boat onto a small raft that kept the driver afloat until he could be picked up by another motorboat.

In the meantime, the motorboat continued toward the target where it crashed and sank. At a predetermined depth the TNT exploaded, sinking the ship. It was one of these boats whose propellers we had seen in Haifa Port.

Since there were too many prying eyes along the Mediterranean coast, it had been decided to do the training on the Sea of Galilee at night. There I met Yohai Bin Nun, the head of the unit, and also Aldo, an Italian, who had served in the Italian Navy and was an expert on their use. (His real name was Fiorenzo Capriotio.) Yossie informed me that four of these were to be mounted on the afterdeck of the *Maoz* and would I please take whatever measurements that were needed so that I could arrange this in the next week, or two.

Such surprise weapons are very often of use the first time only. Afterward, the enemy knows what to expect and can take defensive measures. Apparently, the first time these were used in World War II, the Italians had some success; however, in later battles, such as the one at Malta, these were not successful. In any case, for us these boats were ideal and the most important feature was that we at last had a real naval weapon.

The trip back was equally hair-raising as the trip out, but after deciding that this would be may my last night on earth, I fell asleep only to be awakened when we arrived back in Haifa.

Preparations for the motorboats was quite straightforward. First, a scrounging tour of the refugee ships tied up along the breakwater to find four davits that would lift the boats from their cradles and swing them over the side of the ship. We soon found just what was needed and a crew went to collect these.

The only other bit of equipment needed were some special pelican hooks that are special types of quick release hooks that would drop the boats into the water. Since such items were unknown in Israel and we did not have a blacksmith who could make such a hook, I designed a new type of pelican hook made of steel plates welded together that left only one very major problem.

Several weeks before, the personnel department had sent me a genuine naval architect from Europe who had come as a volunteer. I had put him in charge of the hull repair unit, but almost immediately something seemed all wrong. He was constantly involved in wild arguments with the workshop people, with him insisting on various things that they thought inappropriate.

In a number of cases these situations were brought back to me and in each case I couldn't help but agree with the workshop people. Then one day I decided to make a quiet test, and asked our hull expert to make a sketch of a top mast for the *Eilat*. For some reason the *Eilat* had lost her top mast that was needed to support the signal's yard arm and some antennae. A very simple job, but when the sketch was submitted there was no question in my mind that our expert was not what he was supposed to be.

Then out of the blue came a letter—in English—to me from a very respected member of the community about this particular volunteer. The letter pointed out that he had been a known collaborator with the Nazis and asked how we could employ him in such a trusted position.

I was very much concerned so I went to see Naval Intelligence to discuss how we should handle this. To my further surprise they showed me a letter they had received from Air Force Intelligence more or less covering the contents of my letter. "What to do?" "Don't do anything; we want to watch him." Very easy to say, but not so easy to carry out.

In a properly organized military force such a thing couldn't happen, but one should remember that nothing was organized in Israel at that time. The country had only been in existence a few months and the entire scene was chaotic.

Fortunately, a new volunteer—Hal Notarius—had just arrived from the United States. He was an engineer, a graduate of Cornell, and had been an ensign on a large ship in the U.S. Navy during the war. Hal was a very easygoing sort and seemed to have a sound engineering background, so he was made assistant hull repair officer.

The big question was how do we handle mounting our most secret weapon when the man to be in charge of the operation might well be working for the other side? Fortunately, we had a week before concrete action had to be taken to give Intelligence their chance. Then one day word came that the boats would be delivered in two days—something had to be done.

My next-door neighbor—Avram Ofer—happened to be head of naval personnel and on seeing him on the street that evening I stopped him and explained the urgency of getting this man out of the maspenah immediately. I was very concerned and made it clear that I wouldn't continue waiting for Intelligence to make up their minds.

To my surprise he whipped out a pad of personnel movement orders, and on the spot filled one out and gave it to me, saying, "Have him report to the navy camp at Bat Galim first thing in the morning."

The next day I presented the orders and it did become a bit awkward when he suggested that I could demand that personnel rescind the order, since this had happened a number of times and I had always gotten away with it. However, I explained that in this case there was nothing to be done. So he left and I never heard another word from him or about the incident.

In any case, Hal Notarius took over and the davits were mounted on the *Maoz* and anchors for the boat's cradles fastened to the decks. The night before the ship sailed, in the middle of October, the boats were placed onto the deck ready for action.

It was about this time, the end of September, that the navy received a new ship, the ex-U.S.S. *Yucatan*, a PC boat from U.S. surplus. The formalities had somehow been arranged and a small group of ex-U.S. Navy personnel sailed it to Israel. The most important contribution of the *Yucatan* was Jonny Leff, who was one of the crew. Jonny was an Annapolis graduate, had been a lieutenant on a battleship, and a specialist in gunnery. During the following weeks he was a very very busy fellow.

Unfortunately, this ship had broken a tie rod—one of several long boltlike rods that hold the engine together—during the journey to Israel and arrived with one cylinder out of action. We managed to replace this and put the ship back into action, but the engines were a continuous source of trouble.

Around the tenth of October all hell broke loose, for our long-expected guns arrived. These were genuine Italian naval guns from World War I. There were two three-inch guns and two four-inch guns for the ships and another two guns to be mounted on the beach for training.

Normally this would not have been a particularly complex job, but our orders were to complete the work in only three days, for the fighting was expected to begin any minute.

This did seem somewhat odd, for although the papers mentioned gross breaches of the truce each day, one had a feeling that the truce would persist and there were stories in the news supporting this option as well.

On the sixth, Leonard Bernstien gave an all-Beethoven concert. On the seventh, the S.S. *Negba* brought 426 children to Israel. These were largely orphans, but some were children whose parents sent them on ahead to start a new life. A number of children's villages had been set up to accommodate them. These certainly would not seem to be the sort of activities that precede the outbreak of hostilities.

In any case, our orders were quite clear. The design department's plans were not complete, but the calculations had been finished, and with sketches we were able to start work. One crew went to all the workshops in the industrial area looking for one-inch plate that was to be used on the reinforcement of the decks. Fortunately, this was found at Teifer and Knopf, one of the workshops with which we had excellent relations. It was particularly gratifying at the time for them to offer anything they had on the spot with the formalities to be arranged later.

Then started three days of nonstop work. We recruited all the help we could get. One crew with a welding machine was brought up from Jaffa; contractors were also employed on various parts of the job. Since the final plans were not finished, several of the draftsmen worked together with the workshop people explaining details of the work as they went along. Everyone literally worked until they couldn't go on.

When I had been a student at MIT, Professor Paul Pigors had once mentioned that if one wanted to really know what sort of personality one had, one should go without sleep for twenty-four hours. After twenty-four hours, he maintained, one's real personality would show through. In this case I went three nights without sleep and I guess my real personality did materialize. Tired, very very tired.

During this period every part of the navy was frantically preparing. Jonny Leff had to train gun crews with the two guns mounted on shore. Since no one else had experience in his speciality, every piece of ammunition had to be checked out personally.

Aboard the ships, engine room crews together with maspenah personnel were making last minute efforts to button up engines and make ready for sea. While crews below decks were completing the welding of the structural supports, above decks the guns were first bolted onto their new mounts and then service platforms built so the crews could tend the guns.

When the final morning arrived there were finishing touches still to be added, but the ships were essentially finished.

The *Hagana* and *Wedgewood* each had genuine naval guns, a bit antique perhaps, but these were the real thing. The *Maoz* had its four explosive motorboats carefully placed the preceding night and these had been wrapped with tarpaulins so that their secret was safe.

Then came a short test cruise of several hours to test equipment, especially the new guns. Each gun was fired three times, starboard, port, and the forward gun forward, and the after gun astern. Nothing broke loose so the ships returned to drop off the maspenah crews and left for sea. I went to sleep.

# 15
# The Navy Goes to War

The next week was a confused jumble of events. The Egyptians were entrenched in the Gaza Strip and were a serious threat to the settlements south of Tel Aviv; hence there was a very urgent need to drive them back. Much as predicted, the truce ended and the logical approach to dislodge the Egyptians was from the sea.

The very first action of the "new" fleet under Paul Shulman was a shore bombardment of the enemy along the Gaza Strip. Allan's account of this was told in a somewhat humorous vein. Apparently, after the first salvos, each of the new guns began to exhibit its own personality. One would fire as soon as the breach block was slammed home. Another had to be hit with a hammer to make it fire.

These odd and highly irregular procedures soon became routine. It should be remembered that this was really a makeshift fleet with amateur crews and after the first few salvos the question arose: Were they merely tearing up the beach, or were they causing damage to the Egyptian positions? As Allan later put it, "The crews had never really practiced firing and even if they were only plowing up the sand it was worthwhile practice, so we continued the bombardment. Intelligence reports later showed that the action had indeed been worthwhile.

After this action the ships returned for some minor repairs and a briefing on the next phase. It was after this briefing that Jonny said to me, "I've been scared in action before, but this is the first time I've been scared before the ship left the dock. You should have heard the questions."

This little incident truly symbolizes the real situation. As a basis of comparison during World War II, the U.S. Navy had to be built literally overnight, but this was an overnight of several years with the full backing of the U.S. industrial might. Despite the press of time, ships were put to sea with proper guns; radar; fire control gear; and most important, fully trained crews.

American recruits were sent to boot camps or officers' courses, then later to specialist courses. Finally, on a shakedown cruise each ship with a nucleus of trained crews was put through rigorous training exercises with experts standing by each member of the crew to insure a most intensive education.

In Israel 1948 the situation was literally another world. The ships were resurrected junk with antique guns and no fire control gear. Crews more often than not, had never been to sea before their first battle. Experts could be counted on the fingers of one hand.

Despite this appalling situation the ships did a proper job. To be sure, the ex-merchant marine officers and men who had smuggled illegal immigrants asked naive questions at the briefings and really were out of their class, but they did do the job.

During this same week there was an engagement between the *Hagana, Wedgewood,* and *Nogah* and an enemy corvette. Since the *Nogah* had no heavy guns it withdrew and was promptly attacked by enemy Spitfires. In this phase of the battle one Spitfire was shot down and the *Nogah* was slightly damaged by splinters of exploding bombs.

Meanwhile, the *Hagana* and *Wedgewood* attacked the corvette and although no hits were scored, the enemy withdrew. Later, the ships were under fire from shore batteries and did suffer some superficial damage.

Late that night I received an emergency call that ships had been hit and were lying off Jaffa where the Jaffa base crew were busy applying steel "Band-Aids." When I reached Jaffa, things could not have been under better control.

Standard items in a warship's damage control supplies are tapered wooden plugs to drive into holes made by enemy fire. Weeks before, one of the first things we had done was to supply each ship with a goodly supply of these plugs and there they were. Each ship had a dozen or so pimples sticking out where the plugs protruded.

Fortunately, no shells had exploded in the ships and these holes were quickly covered with patches and by morning the ships were again at sea.

A few hours later it was learned that the Egyptians had sent their flagship, the *King Farouk,* and a minesweeper to Gaza, and with the coming of night the *Maoz* sailed toward Gaza. It was decided that two of the explosive motorboats piloted by Zallman Abramov and Yaacov Vardi would each attack a ship, while Yohai Bin Nun—the commander of the unit—would follow to attack any remaining target. A fourth boat operated by Yizhac Brookman and Yaacov Ritov was to follow and pick up the crews from their rafts after their boats had exploded. A simple plan, but as in all battle plans, there were surprises.

Once launched, the first two boats ended up both attacking the *King Farouk,* which was sunk. However, the mechanisms that were to release the pilots with their rafts did not work and each had a problem getting free from their boats.

By this time, the minesweeper was fully alerted and as Yohai went in to attack he found himself not only under fire from machine guns, but illuminated by the ship's searchlight. Despite the danger, he pressed his attack and like the two preceding attackers, found that his escape mechanism did not work. He too had a struggle getting free of the boat and only managed to hit the water twenty meters from the minesweeper.

Fortunately, the explosives all worked and both ships were sunk. Picking up the three pilots who were left swimming in the water also presented difficulties, since their caps, equipped with infrared lights, were all lost. But the motorboat managed to pick up all three and shortly thereafter they were back on the *Maoz*.

To a great extent the events of these few days decided the naval war. The Egyptians were quite amazed at the power of this infant navy, less than three months old. We, too, learned some valuable lessons. The ships' guns were not really very effective, and in the long run there would have to be some very serious changes.

# 16
# Settling Down

The next month and half of 1948 our lives were a strange dichotomy. On the one hand we were up to our necks in a war but on the other, the Gershoni household was approaching some sort of normality. We read newspaper headlines such as the following and were somehow reassured:

| | |
|---|---|
| 1 November | Cease Fire in Galilee |
| 1 November | Army of North Drives Kaukji Out of the Country |
| 7 November | Migdal Pocket Falls to Jews |
| 19 November | Beduin Sheikhs Sue for Peace |

These headlines seemed to imply that the army was able to defend the country. At the same time we were also seeing much less ominous stories in our papers that also strengthened our optimism.

| | |
|---|---|
| 3 November | The Hebrew National Opera presents the Barber of Seville (Advertisement) |
| 9 November | Israel Takes First Census |
| 19 November | Air Company Formed [El-Al] |
| 19 November | All Israel to Be Vaccinated |
| 25 November | Lydda Back in Action |
| 17 December | Telephone Line Links Jerusalem with Coast |

Of course there were also the usual sorts of everyday occurrences like robberies and an occasional murder; these always brought the same comment. "Now we're a normal country like any other."

Thus, from such news items one can see that amid our military worries there was a certain amount of normality creeping into our lives. Moreover, we had the feeling that the country was beginning to operate as a modern state.

By this time the navy was functioning, even though it was still a pretty makeshift outfit. The ships went to sea and did their jobs. Those of us ashore began to consolidate our facilities. Our navy yard was rapidly becoming a well-equipped organization capable of handling virtually every sort of repair.

Up until this time we had been working seven days a week, ten to twelve hours a day, and this had to come to an end for everyone, particularly for those in responsible positions who were completely exhausted. During World War II it had been found in both the United States and the United Kingdom that people working seven-day weeks actually produced less then when they worked shorter hours. Israel in 1948 seemed to be following the same pattern.

I personally found that at this pace I could just keep things running, but it was extremely difficult to plan anything new. Thus, one day we decided to honor Shabat each week—we began to work a six-day week, and this was another big step toward normality.

Life on the home front was also due for a change. For the first few weeks the Gershonis had been living in the Ben Yehuda Hotel and this was certainly a pleasant expedient. Little David used to eat all his meals in the dining room and accepted this new way of life as completely normal. He also got used to having a father again. However, nice as this was, we really began to miss having our own home.

During this interim period Marilyn and Davy began to meet new friends and see a bit of Haifa, which was really worth seeing, for Haifa is truly one of the world's most beautiful cities. The city itself at the time, was pretty shabby, with gardens untended and houses needing paint. Moreover, in certain areas such as the French Carmel, and near the port, rusted barbed wire was still very much in evidence. This was of course the result of World War II and then the trouble that arose as the British pulled out of Palestine. However, despite the shabby apperance, Haifa had great natural beauty.

Mount Carmel rises out of the sea and Haifa is built up, its sides overlooking the Mediterranean and Haifa Bay. One of the first things to impress me about the view is that the Mediterranean is so very blue, almost like a painting.

The lowest level near the port was devoted to all sorts of commercial enterprises and the Arab quarter. Halfway up the mountain was the main residential and shopping area, and then at the top was a small shopping center and some very lovely residential quarters.

The big event for the Gershonis was the day our car and lift with our furniture arrived. The car, as with all new immigrants of military age, was immediately inducted into the army. This was pretty much the norm for any vehicle of recent vintage. As with all new recruits it was given a nice khaki uniform and a military number. In this particular case the car was then issued back to me.

The navy assigned us an apartment in "Bevingrad," which was the name then used for the last stronghold of the British before they left Palestine. As the areas under their control began to shrink, the British fortified their remaining positions. Thus around the port of Haifa was not just a fence, but a mammoth barbed wire affair fifty feet high. Bevingrad, the French Carmel, had a much more modest array of rusted entanglements and it was months before these disappeared.

The French Carmel, named after a number of French monasteries still located there, was a residential section on top of the mountain that had been largely occupied by senior British officials. Our new home at Four Bashir Street had been occupied by a British official until the very end of their occupation and then it and the entire area was simply abandoned.

The house was an attractive stone building that had been sub-divided into several apartments. The living room was quite special since it was two stories high—impossible to heat in the winter but quite lovely the rest of the year. One whole wall was entirely windows with the usual Middle Eastern shutters that could be lowered for privacy and protection from intruders.

Our new bedroom had been a sun room in the past and had a large balcony ideal for children's play. What had once been the dining room became the children's room despite the fact that two of them would not arrive for several years.

The bathroom and separate toilet were typical of Israel at that time, but somewhat strange to us spoiled Americans. Hot water was supplied by a "geyser." This was a vertical tank at the end of the bathtub fitted with a container for kerosene on the wall. When one wanted to take a shower, a small valve was opened allowing the kerosene to drip down a pipe to the burner under the water tank. Once lit, the geyser growled or roared according to how much you had opened the valve and in about twenty minutes there was plenty of hot water for a shower or bath.

Every few days the kerosene man would appear on the corner with his tank of kerosene mounted on two wheels and pulled by a donkey. All the neighbors would line up with their jerricans to buy kerosene for the same system was used in most houses. Within a very short time we were also to find that most people used kerosene for cooking as well.

Our kitchen was quite unique in those days. First of all we had a real refrigerator. This was very special, for most of the neighbors had iceboxes and the ice was brought to the neighborhood by much the same technique as the kerosene. The ice wagon was pulled by donkey and when the iceman arrived, he blew a horn and everyone lined up and took home a block of ice to keep their food cool.

European as well as Israeli voltage is two hundred twenty volts instead of the American standard of one hundred twenty; hence a transformer was necessary. This minor conversion was quite satisfactory, but our stove was another matter entirely.

The stove was a brand-new electric model that we soon learned required more current than was available to the entire building; hence, we had to have it rewired. Finaly, after some of the experts from the maspenah finished the conversion, two small burners were usable. Needless to say, we were somewhat disappointed. So after a few days I decided that I ought to change things around a bit.

I spent an entire afternoon rewiring the stove to make it more functional. Then about eight o'clock, long after dark, I decided to try it out. Suddenly, there was a tremendous crash and the house, the building, and the entire neighborhood was without electricity.

Fortunately, someone called the electric company and word soon got around the neighborhood that the servicemen were on their way. In the meantime, I frantically disconnected the stove and rewired it as it had been. What the penalty was for such stupidity I could not imagine. However, the men from the electric company arrived, changed the fuse on top of the pole outside the house, and then left without asking any questions. Apparently this sort of thing happened all the time.

It was not long, however, until we changed over to a local method of cooking. In those days people used small primus single-burner cookers that were frightening affairs. These burned kerosene and had to be pumped up before using. The more modern homes had simple kerosene stoves. Thus on top of our very elaborate American electric stove there soon appeared a two-burner kerosene stove that served us for years.

For the next few weeks it seemed that the place was completely filled with boxes and barrels. With time, however, the place became home. The lift van—the huge box that had contained our belongings, was sold, for this was a very useful commodity. In fact, there was a tiny synagogue on the Carmel made from such a lift.

In order to help Marilyn get settled, we managed to hire a woman who, like almost everyone we met, had a story to tell. She was a beautiful and very sophisticated woman very much out of place doing housework but, she was a new immigrant trying to make a new start and not afraid of work. There was, however, one thing that she insisted that she could not do, and that was to answer the doorbell.

The story then came out that in Europe her husband had been taken by the Gestapo and the local commander made it known to her that if she wanted to see her husband alive again she would have to be very nice to the head of the Gestapo. As she put it, she simply was not up to opening the door and perhaps one day meeting an old acquaintance.

She left us after a very short time and her replacement also had a story to tell. Juliette was an Arab girl about eighteen and when she first came to us she had a bandage around her ankle. Marilyn asked what was wrong and she told the following story.

Apparently, just before the British left, a convoy appeared in her village and the British soldiers insisted that everyone board the trucks and leave their homes. It was explained that when the Arabs from the surrounding countries invaded there would be so much violence and bloodshed that it would be better for everyone to leave for a short while. In this way they would not be in the way of the invading armies and they could soon return after the country had been taken from the Jews.

Juliette had other ideas, however. She had a boyfriend in Haifa and refused to leave. Whereupon she was thrown bodily onto the truck and driven away from her home. Being young, in love, and determined, she waited until the truck slowed down along the route and jumped off, breaking her ankle.

We heard this same story of forcing residents to leave to avoid the fighting over and over again. In this case, however, we heard the story from someone who was there. Juliette was a very lovely girl who was part of our immediate family group for about four years and we never had any reason to doubt her word.

The view held then, which still seems the only reasonable explanation of the British behavior, is that the British abandoned the country with a view of returning. They seemed to feel that if they left, the Arab armies would overrun the country. Then, when the Jewish population had been reduced to a few pockets of Jews desperately trying to hold off the surrounding hoards, the civilized world would demand that they return to restore order.

While our home life seemed to be settling down, and the military side of our life seemed at least dormant, another factor, political activity, began to stew. Since the pot would boil over during the next month, let's look at some of the political headlines, for with hindsight they help to explain some of the events of the next month of 1948.

17 November     10 Airmen Face Trial on Arms Smuggling Charges

23 November     Arab Armies Reequipped Now prepared to throw
                Jews out of Palestine

30 November     150,000 British Troops Still in Canal Zone

5 December      Britain to Train Yemen Pilots
                Saudi Pilots to Train in U.S.

9 December      British Threat

10 December     Britain Seeks Excuse for Army to Operate in
                Negev

16 December     British Arms Reached Arabs During Truce

In essence, these headlines all centered around the basic issue that
Britain, despite having given up her mandate in Palestine, was not
only interested in returning, but was also prepared to take military
action.

On the one hand there was an embargo of arms to Israel that was
enforced in the United States, but on the other hand, Britain was
openly arming the Arab states. Moreover, on 9 December the British
government stated that they would step in militarily if the situation
warranted such action. It was not long before we saw that this threat
was not an idle one.

Abandoned immigrant ships along Haifa Port breakwater. The ship with the black smokestack in the background is the *Exodus*.

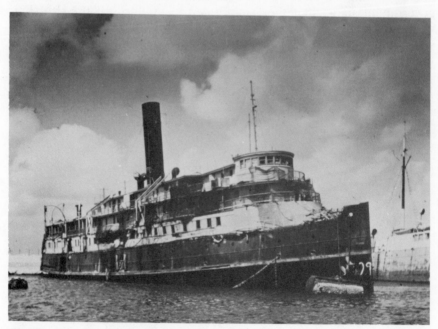

The *Exodus*, abandoned with the other refugee ships along the Haifa breakwater.

Davy, Marilyn, Vic, and Judy Avrunin.

**Davy enjoying the wild flowers on Mount Carmel.**

Officers of the navy yard. *Standing, from left (second)* Steuer; *(third)* Novick; *(fifth)* Gershoni; *(ninth)* Krauss; *kneeling (left)* Notarius.

The corner grocery on Mount Carmel.

The author.

The author and Davy.

Davy at the antisniper wall in Jerusalem.

Jerusalem water truck. Used to distribute water after the pumping station supplying the city was destroyed.

Refugees coming home.

Last of the Cyprus detainees arriving in Haifa.

Aluminum huts in the new city of Kiryat Shmona. Note the barber shop.

Simha at "Dok" Israel Precision Foundries.

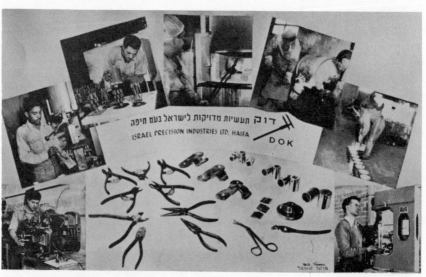

Selection of "Dok's" products surrounded by pictures of the precision casting process.

# 17
# Five Spitfires

It looked like things had really cooled off along the various fronts and we saw in our papers of 19 December that there was quiet on all fronts. This, our first Christmas season in Israel, was a minor shock after so many years of Christmas in the United States. We thoroughly enjoyed the Israeli version completely devoid of festivities. Aside from a small note in the papers that Christian members of the armed forces would be given leave, this period was no different than any other.

Why would this quiet Christmas appeal to us? Being the only Jew in the class had often been unpleasant and Christmas for the lone Jew was quite a trial. In those days it was considered quite appropriate for the schools and the community to make quite a thing of the Christmas holidays and we could not help but feel most uncomfortable being so much involved in a holiday that was not part of our religion. Hence, the great appreciation of the Israeli version—we were at home.

Unfortunately, this calm was not to last. On 22 December fighting broke out in the Negev, a large operation that included the navy. Essentially, the navy's task was to blockade the Gaza coast to keep the Egyptian fleet away. The Egyptians did make an attempt to approach the coast and bombard Israeli troops, but the Israeli Navy drove them off.

During this period we got our taste of the war in Haifa too, for on the twenty-sixth, Haifa and Tel Aviv had air raids. Somewhere behind our house there was an antiaircraft battery that went into action one night, but I slept through the firing. The first thing I knew about the action was when Marilyn grabbed me. By this time the firing was over and she told me what happened. We waited to see if there would be more firing, but all was quiet and we were soon back asleep.

In essence, the battle in the Negev was highly successful and our forces were able to break the Egyptian hold on the southern coastal region. This was, of course, great news, but the interesting part of the action was only told to us some weeks later when we saw Benny and Ora Aden.

At that time, the Egyptian forces were like two long arms thrust into

Israeli territory, one toward Bir Asluj on the road to Beersheba, and the other toward Gaza. This second thrust was dependent on the sea for support. Their objective was to bring the two arms together, thereby pinching off the Jewish settlements in the south.

Benny was a senior officer in the brigade in Beersheba, and his unit was endeavoring to throw the Egyptians out of Israel. Their main problem was how to get from Beersheba to the coast so as to engage the Egyptian forces. Since the country between Beersheba and the coast was completely impassable wilderness, this looked like an impossible task.

However, one of the scholars in the unit remembered reading about a Roman road from Beersheba to Auja el Hafir near the coast. Apparently in ancient times another army had moved over the same route to the sea. One must remember that Israelis feel a very strong bond with the past; thus, such a solution was most attractive.

It was certainly worth a try, so scouts in a jeep were sent to see what they could find and some hours later they returned jubilant. There really was a way to the sea and definite signs of an ancient Roman road. This hitherto unknown road seemed to be the perfect solution, so Benny and a few others went out to make sure it was passable. The ancient roadway seemed to be adequate so the decision was made to try and get through to the sea by this ancient route.

As Benny explained, the Roman road soon became useless and every truck had to be moved through the sandy waste with two bulldozers—one pushing and one pulling. The noise seemed to be so loud that they were sure that the Egyptians would discover them. However, no attack came and the unit was soon on the coastal road behind the Egyptians. Then, just at breakfast time, they stormed into the Egyptian positions from behind, taking them completely by surprise. After this overwhelming defeat, the Egyptians felt their position to be hopeless and literally ran away.

Apparently, our success in the Negev was giving the British some anxious moments and they were having serious misgivings about their decision to leave the country, for in early 1949 we began to see headlines such as:

| | |
|---|---|
| 5 January | Britain Landing Troops in Akaba |
| 6 January | Active U.K. Intervention Still Possible |
| 6 January | Britain Seen as Real Enemy |
| 9 January | Military Stores Flown In (to Amman) |
| 9 January | Brits Taking Steps to Safeguard Their Interests |

9 January   RAF Flying Patrols over Sinai

9 January   British Fleet to Mediterranean

Then the headlines showed that the British were serious and not posturing appeared.

6 January   Five British Planes Shot Down Over Israel as Cease-Fire Goes into Effect in Negev

6 January   Two RAF Pilots Captured Well Inside Frontier

Suddenly, the whole situation took a very serious turn from optimism to concern, since fighting the entire Arab world was one thing, but fighting the British with our makeshift forces was another matter entirely.

By chance, we had invited a large group of friends over that evening. As was the custom, everyone brought along their friends, and we soon had a crowd of over fifty. Most of them were in the armed forces and we had representatives from many countries: South Africa, England, Canada, Maylasia, New Zealand, and the United States. Since there were volunteers from over fifty countries in the Israeli Army, this was nothing special.

Obviously, the main topic of conversation was the five Spits and what was going to happen. With every new broadcast we all sat around the radio, mainly on the floor, and tried to make sense out of the various reports from all over the world. It certainly seemed as if we were on our way to fighting the British. Then around midnight a very concerned group left for home, wondering if we really would be at war with the British the following day.

The Gershonis straightened up the flat and went to sleep, but it was not to be for long. At about three o'clock the doorbell rang and I managed to stagger to the door. There stood a messenger from headquarters with a large brown envelope sealed in wax. I signed his receipt and asked him to wait until I saw what this was all about.

Inside the envelope was its twin brother, also sealed with wax. Finally, I extracted a document, in Hebrew. What damn fool woke me in the middle of the night with a Hebrew message; everyone knew that my knowledge of the language was limited to about twenty words.

There was no alternative but to give the messenger the letter and ask him to tell me what it was all about. He glanced at the paper, turned white, and muttered that I had better get someone to translate it for me. By this time I was fully awake and very much concerned. Since one of our neighbors was "Kippy" Kaplan, the captain of one of our corvettes, he seemed like the best available translator.

A couple of minutes later "Kippy" was standing in the doorway reading like mad in Hebrew and muttering phrases in English.

. . . British dropping paratroops in Negev . . .

. . . amphibious landing Natanya to cut country in two . . .

. . . armored assault from Akaba . . .

. . . naval bombardment of coastal cities . . .

This was the one and only time my hair began to stand on end. What could be done with our facilities against such forces? Suddenly, I realized that there was one thing missing, and I interrupted the soliloquy. "Kippy, has this happened, is it happening, or is it going to happen?" Whereupon Kippy muttered, "Shut up, I'm reading," and continued his bilingual performance. Suddenly he burst out laughing and said, "Go back to bed; some idiot thinks that this might happen, and he just wanted to be sure you knew."

The next few days were anxious ones with reports such as "British Dig in Around Akaba," and "$200,000,000 Worth of British Arms Sent to Egyptians." With time it became clear that there were influential forces within the British government that were not prepared to leave the Middle East, and that they were doing everything they could to find a way to stay.

An Associated Press report from Cyprus—the British Headquarters in the Middle East—appeared in the Palestine Post on the tenth, presenting what was thought to be the official British line of thought. It explained that peace talks were doomed as long as the Jews insisted on retaining the Negev, since Britain felt that it could not let a nation she felt antagonistic, to remain on sand that was a protective barrier to the canal and Akaba.

The article went on to cite all sorts of supposed mineral wealth to be found in the Negev and indicated that the British were reluctant to give this up. The article concluded with, "If the Jews had been content to leave both alone (the Negev and Akaba) they might now be enjoying the peace they claim to yearn for."

One particular incident that caused many smiles was when the British government attempted to send a letter of protest to the Israeli government. Since they did not recognize Israel, the letter was sent to the "Jewish Authorities in Tel Aviv." The letter was returned by the postal authorities with an appropriate comment that such an addressee was unknown.

At first the British papers were antagonistic to Israel, but gradually as more facts were uncovered, the mood began to change. Finally, the obvious question was asked. Why were British planes over a battle area, when Britain was not at war?

Suddenly, as if a balloon had burst, the British press was attacking their government and the initial animosity disappeared to be replaced by powerful attacks on the British policy in the Middle East. The *Observer* expressed these views in an editorial. "To say that it is aggression on Israel's part when she reoccupies the Negev allocated to her by the General Assembly's partition resolution and invaded by Egypt would be tantamount to declaring the resolution null and void."

Suddenly the entire political climate changed. Israel was suddenly recognized by a number of countries such as Canada, Argentina, Sweden, Peru, and Italy, which had been dragging their feet on this issue. Then on 19 January Bevin announced that the Jews still held in British concentration camps in Cyprus would be released to continue their journey to Israel. Over 11,800 Jews were still languishing in Cyprus and there had been repeated attempts to get the British to release them, all to no avail. Then suddenly this radical about turn.

The following weeks saw the S.S. *Galila* and the S.S. *Atzmaut* in Haifa harbor, unloading these thousands of now bewildered immigrants. Most could not believe what was happening when suddenly they were put aboard these Jewish ships flying the Israeli flag and brought to freedom and a new life. The last ship from Cyprus arrived in Haifa on 11 February and received a tumultuous welcome. Bands playing, flags flying, Israeli troops on parade, and their own people to help them start new lives.

As the ship came alongside the quay, "Hatikva" was played and everyone stood to attention. At this dramatic moment I noticed out of the corner of my eye a French motor whaleboat from one of the truce observer's destroyers and in it, their sailors standing at attention. I couldn't resist the urge to photograph this, for it seemed to symbolize what was happening.

There was not a dry eye in the entire port, and even after almost forty years the memory of the scene brings back its tears.

This short period brought a whole jumble of events each showing the world that Israel was real and here to stay. On the twenty-fifth of January we had elections for the first constituent assembly and it was noted in the press that there were Arab lists of candidates and that 69,000 Arabs would have the first chance in their lives to vote.

We read that the German DP camps were to be closed and 40,000 of the 65,000 Jews still left, were coming to Israel. Similarly, the camp in Aden was to be closed and another 4,000 Yemenite Jews were soon due. These were heady days, for these events were what it was all about. After 2,000 years the Jewish State was truly in business, looking after its own.

# 18
# Tourists

After the furor of events associated with Spitfires and the camps in Cyprus, the character of the news changed radically as did our whole lives. Here and there the military situation would flare up, but these were always small local affairs. Our war of survival was over, and a form of peace began to evolve.

On 24 February, after six weeks of negotiations on the Isle of Rhodes, Egypt and Israel signed an armistice. Then followed similar armistices with Lebanon, on 27 March, and Trans-Jordan on 4 April. These were not peace treaties, for it was thought that the final treaties would require a few more months of negotiations. No one at this time anticipated that real peace might well take generations. Israel was also accepted as a member of the United Nations on 13 May, just a few days after her first birthday.

Locally we were all proud of the fact that Israel's first parliament opened on 15 May with the election of our first president, Chaim Weizmann. This was a very exciting time, but one will note that these events were all spaced weeks apart. Between these historic dates were all sorts of minor events that gave character to our daily living.

The maspenah was now an accepted fact of life in Haifa Port. So much so, that our navy yard became the center of a minor political battle. There were several ship repair firms in the area that had been contractors for the British Navy and then later for the Israeli Navy. However, these were mainly outside the port and much smaller than the maspenah. Now that peace had more or less arrived, there was talk of turning the navy yard over to one of these more than anxious firms.

Acquiring such a facility that could also be used for commercial ship repairs would have been a very attractive business, but not at all practical for the navy. At this same time a large American consulting firm was called in to assist in modernizing the port. They were somehow or other drawn into the controversy and in due course the local representative of this firm made an appointment to meet with the head of the navy yard.

It must be remembered that Israel was a very young country and many of its officials and senior officers were also very young in many cases much much younger than their foreign counterparts. In this case the results were rather humorous.

The port consultant had seen and heard all about the maspenah, and on being shown into my office he took one look at me and blurted out: "You're in charge here?" I assured him that he was in the right place and we began to discuss the plans for the new port.

Being an American expert and considerably older than I, he began to explain to me all sorts of nonsense on how navy yards were run in America. In essence he wanted to turn the navy facilities over to a civilian company, claiming that this was the way it was done in the United States.

Since I was not supposed to be American, I could not come right out and contradict his misinformation, but I did mention that such a system would not be practical for a military facility and suggested that if he checked he would find that U.S. navy yards employed civilians, but were very much controlled by the navy.

This concept seemed to spoil his plans, and as he began to present his rebuttal, his gaze fell on my U.S. Navy raincoat, hanging behind my desk. Suddenly, the dawn seemed to break when he put two and two together—my accent and the American navy raincoat. After a pause he said, "Well, perhaps you know more about these things than I do." The subject was then dropped.

About this time Vic became involved in a most interesting operation that had far-reaching effects. Private automobiles were very rare in Israel, and the overwhelming majority of the population did not know how to drive. Thus, with the influx of military vehicles and thousands of new and inexperienced drivers, the number of traffic accidents literally soared.

The results were catastrophic. People were being killed and disabled on the roads and vehicles, desperately needed for the army, were being destroyed. The country simply could not tolerate such losses. Then one day Vic was summoned to see the Old Man—Ben Gurion. Ben Gurion outlined the situation and indicated that he wanted Vic to take charge of an accident prevention program. Vic agreed to take charge but, with his usual chutzpah, agreed with one condition. He insisted that there would be no outside interference.

Ben Gurion agreed, and they decided to call the operation Mivzah Mordechai ("Operation Mordechai"), after Colonel Mordechai Zimzabi who had recently been killed in a road accident.

Vic's approach was original and astonishingly effective. First, he published new speed limits for the army of 55 kilometers per hour—36 miles per hour—outside the city, and 35 kilometers per hour—23 miles per hour—within built-up areas. The army was then informed that this would be rigidly enforced with speed traps. Moreover, at the site of every speed trap would be a military court to try violators on the spot.

The main penalty would be time in a labor camp with no exceptions for rank. The vehicle would also be impounded so the unit of the speeding driver would be doubly penalized, the loss of the vehicle and the loss of the driver.

Then Vic made sure that everyone knew he meant business. In this regard all sorts of stories circulated about senior officers who had been caught. At first it was very odd driving so slowly, but after a very short time one got used to this. It was very relaxing to travel about the country, and I don't recall that the additional time on the road was particularly noticeable. The startling thing, however, was that immediately the accident rate of hundreds a month dropped to almost nothing. Unfortunately, however, after some months of success the program was discontinued.

One thing that was apparent to the Gershonis was that we had to learn Hebrew. On a day-to-day basis we could get along, for everyone we knew spoke English; however, it was obvious that we could not really become integrated into the community without knowing the language of the country.

The navy was very pleased to assign a young man, Haim, to not only teach us Hebrew, but also to show us some of the country. Haim struggled valiantly to teach us Hebrew, but I'm sure he never anticipated such a completely inept student as myself. Where I grew up in the middle of Illinois there was only one language, English. Not only did none of my buddies know another language, but we never ever heard one.

There was a recent immigrant in our school who spoke Italian at home, and we were convinced that he must be a genius, for he spoke "two" languages.

Actually, for people with such a background, and also without a facility for learning languages, Hebrew can be a long-term task. One has to make learning the language a way of life to be pursued one way or another over many years. The only ray of hope I might extend to the beginner is that after many years I did more or less learn the language. This, in essence, means that anyone can.

Haim's other function, of teaching us something of the country, was a much bigger success. One day he suggested a weekend trip to Jerusalem and this was to be a very special treat. Since the road was known to be very difficult, I took the car to one of the local service stations for a change of oil and lubrication, and here I had another lesson about life in Israel.

To my surprise the very pedantic German proprietor asked if I wanted him to wash the engine and underneath the car. He obviously was not joking and seemed to know what he was about, so I asked him to tell me more about these strange ideas. He then explained that in Israel automobiles were very valuable and if one wanted to take care of his car he ought to wash all the muck off the engine and from underneath so that periodically the car could be checked.

I mentioned that we were off to Jerusalem that afternoon and, since this sounded like a worthwhile thing to do, he should go ahead. When I returned to pick up the car an hour later I found out just how worthwhile it really was. He greeted me with, "I'm afraid that you're not going to Jerusalem today; you've got a broken spring." This seemed completely impossible, for the car had been fine when I drove in to his service station. However, when the car was raised on the hoist, there was no doubt that it was an acccident about to happen. The spring was hanging on by grim determination until I could get it to a garage.

The real problem was what to do? I drove very carefully to the local Dodge agent only to find that there had been no spare parts imported since before World War II. In the United States the old parts of virtually anything are thrown away to be replaced by new ones. Switches, engine parts, handles, virtually everything is replaced, even broken springs of Dodge automobiles. However, due to the lack of replacement parts, this concept was completely unknown in Israel. If something broke, someone fixed it or made another one from scratch.

The Dodge people suggested that I take the car to the local blacksmith around the corner and that he would make a new spring. This sounded very strange, but they assured me that it would be beseder, and since there was no other alternative I went to see the blacksmith. There, in a tiny workshop the size of an American bathroom, was the Jewish equivalent of the village blacksmith. To my amazement, as soon as I explained the problem, he immediately took over with a very professional approach. This guy knew what he was doing.

While I waited, he forged a new spring, carefully heat treated it to give it the proper hardness, and then assembled it to the car. Then off we went to Jerusalem, very much wiser on life in a pioneering country.

The road to Jerusalem certainly lived up to its reputation, for as we left the coastal plane, we encountered numerous shell holes in the road that had not yet been repaired. It seemed that a good bit of the time we were off the road going around these bad spots.

In Hebrew one does not "go to Jerusalem" one goes "up to Jerusalem." One could say that this is because the city is high. However, one must remember that Jerusalem has been the spiritual capital of the Jewish people for thousands of years and since ancient days one went "up" to the holy city.

That is exactly how we felt, and as we began to get glimpses of the city from the road as it wound about the mountains, one indeed had a spiritual feeling. We entered the city at dusk and immediately noticed that all of the buildings were made of Jerusalem stone. Hewn blocks of yellowish white stones, which at sunset took on a gold hue, giving the city a very spiritual aura.

The city itself certainly did look as if it had stood up to a difficult siege with demolished buildings on every side. In fact, few buildings showed no signs of the incessant shelling and sniping.

It was then that we noticed the numerous walls built throughout the city to protect civilians from sniping. For many years to come, long after there was a cease-fire, the Trans-Jordan Legion frequently fired at random at people on the street. Hence, an obvious solution to the problem was to build these walls that shielded the population from view.

In one district, right at the dividing line separating Jewish Jerusalem from no man's land, there was just such a wall, very high and made of sheet metal. If you looked through small holes in this wall you could see the barbed wire and the rubbish of no man's land and in the distance the ancient wall of the Old City. The surprising thing was, that if one turned around, one saw a quiet residential district with a sign on one of the buildings indicating a children's kindergarten.

During the peak of the fighting, people abandoned these areas. However, as new immigrants began to filter into the city and more suitable housing was unavailable, these frontline areas were again occupied. Naturally the local residents attempted to live a normal life, despite the fact that the only thing that protected them from snipers was a sheet metal fence. Thus on one side of the fence was the horror of war, but on the other was a quiet street where people went about their daily lives.

It was along these frontal areas that we saw another sight reminiscent of the early fighting. Our enemies believed that the city could not hold out surrounded as it was by established and vastly more numerous Arab forces. Considering the fact that the main Arab army was the Trans-Jordan Legion, which had been organized, trained, equipped, and led by the British, this was not such an unreasonable idea.

Thus, along the frontlines one saw many burned-out shops where the iron shutters were painted with a crescent or a cross. These signs were to have indicated to the advancing Arabs that the store should be left alone because it was owned by a fellow Arab. Unfortunately for these storekeepers, these areas were fought over many times and Arab liberators were driven off.

We had dinner with Cecil and Anne Hyman and got a firsthand look at how Jerusalemites lived during the siege. We also heard all sorts of stories on how they lived and raised small children under such conditions. Despite all the danger and problems, they had managed to achieve some sort of normality in their daily lives. Cecil had continued to manage Barclays Bank, and Anne was a doctor doing research at Hebrew University.

Anne laughingly told us of one of the children's birthdays when she decided to use a package of chocolate pudding she had been hoarding for just such an occasion. When she began to prepare this special surprise, however, she found that milk, sugar, and eggs were all required by the recipe on the box. Such ingredients had not been seen in Jerusalem for months. So with no alternative, she made the pudding with what she had. She described the results as being pretty grim, but under the circumstances everyone thought the pudding to be a wonderful treat.

The following day we did manage to get a glimpse of the ancient wall around the Old City and to see the Tower of David in the distance, but the old city of Jerusalem was to be closed to Jews for many years to come. However, we did see a bit of the new city during the few hours we were there.

The original wagons for distributing water to the population had been replaced by minitankers, small motorized tank trucks, very much in evidence. Another sight, an omen of things to come, was long lines at food stores. one of the remarkable things about the siege was that despite desperate shortages of food, an extremely rigid system of rationing insured that everyone got his share. Rationing was still in existence in Jerusalem and would shortly be followed by strict rationing in the rest of the country.

This was of course a very quick visit, but seeing Jerusalem and meeting its courageous people added an enormous amount to our feeling for the country. Looking back over the years we have seen that many countries and church groups have made all sorts of claims to Jerusalem. There is no doubt that some religions had their roots in this ancient city. However, it did seem strange that when the chips were down, no one but these crazy Jerusalem Jews would lift a finger to defend the city. The Hymans and their neighbors were prepared to live in the city under the worst of conditions and fight for it. We were proud to be associated with them.

# 19
# Ingathering of the Exiles

How can one relate to headlines such as these of 1948:

7 October     Negba Brings 426 Children

24 October     15,000 Children to Reach Israel in Coming Year

Such stories, of course, concerned the bringing of thousands of Jewish orphans from the camps in Europe to Israel. Today, living as we do in comparative safety, such stories have little meaning. One has to actually see such events for the tragedy to penetrate and take on meaning.

Trusty Haim must have understood this phenomenon, for one afternoon he suggested a visit to a youth village on Mount Carmel. The experience was shocking. Here we saw that youngsters, during the time of Hitler, had been sent off on their own from all over Europe. Many parents had begun to see that it would not be long before they, together with their children, would be taken by the Nazis, so in order to save their children, they sent them away to Palestine to be raised in such villages.

These frantic mothers and fathers really had no way of knowing if the children would indeed reach a safe haven, but their desperation had reached the point where they were prepared to take a desperate chance. It was only when we considered such a situation in terms of our own son that we began to understand the grim reality that had faced so many less fortunate parents.

The village looked to us like a rather modest summer camp with simple athletic grounds and elementary school facilities. Obviously, the budget had been a minimum one, but we could not help but be impressed by the fact that thousands of youngsters had survived the Holocaust because of their parents' iron-willed sacrifice.

This trip to the youth village was perhaps an excellent introduction to a subject that was to occupy a most prominent part of our thinking in the coming years. Although there had been a trickle of new immigrants to Palestine, now a miracle occurred. It was like a flood of people. Every day or so a new ship would arrive in the port. During 1949 we saw headlines such as:

| | |
|---|---|
| 21 March | Half Shanghai's Jews in Israel |
| 23 March | 30,000 in March |
| 24 April | Aden Jews Flying to Israel |
| 8 May | Lebanese Jews to Be Permitted to Come to Israel |
| 15 May | Immigrants at Rate of 300,000 a Year |
| 20 May | Skymasters Fly Jews from India |
| 20 May | 218,000 in First Year |
| 24 May | No Immigrant Rejected |

This massive ingathering was in a sense overwhelming. The streets were like the Tower of Babel. Every conceivable language was spoken. We would see families out for a walk with the two parents talking in one language while the kids spoke Hebrew to each other. Then suddenly one of the children would turn to speak to Momma or Papa in their native language. It was then that the need for a single Israeli language became so very obvious.

One interesting sidelight of this continuous confusion of languages is that one could get along regardless of one's native tongue. If one were on a bus, for example, and asked the driver for directions, chances were he could speak a bit of the foreign language. If not, someone on the bus would step forward to translate. Such incidents were everyday occurrences. Since most Europeans spoke several languages, there was always somebody to help the bewildered newcomer.

Today, of course, such scenes have long since disappeared, for chances are, that the Mommas and Poppas of today are the kids of 1949 and everyone speaks Hebrew.

Our neighbor, Dora Nadler, was from Shanghai and one day she couldn't wait to tell us about a high school chum from Shanghai who had arrived that very day. The friend was an operating theater nurse and on her way to Dora's she had stopped at Elisha Hospital to see if they could use a nurse with her experience. After showing her credentials she found herself, not only with a job, but quarters in the hospital as well. Most immigrants had a much more difficult time.

With time, a very sophisticated program evolved in which the passport officials actually went to the various European ports in order to process the new imigrants on the ship during the journey to Israel. Thus, on the ship's arrival trucks and ambulances were waiting to take the newcomers to transit camps or in many cases to hospitals. Thus the bustle of immigrants with their pitiful bundles of belongings being loaded onto trucks and ambulances, was a daily sight in Haifa Port.

Getting them home to Israel was only the first of a long series of problems. The next major obstacle was what to do with this avalanche of people. At first the immigrants were sent to large transit camps, and *mabarah*—"transit camp"—became a household word. Abandoned British Army Camps were used until they were all packed to capacity. There everyone was given a cot, one blanket, and two sheets, and here they waited until some form of more permanent housing could be arranged.

Shaar Aliyah was one such camp located at the foot of Mount Carmel near where we lived. It was a real horror. From the outside it seemed like a seething mass of humanity surrounded by barbed wire. Here, basic physical examinations were held, for disease was a very real problem. An attempt was also made to sort the newcomers by age, education, family status, special skills, and the possibility of having relatives in Israel so that some form of housing and employment could be provided.

The whole process was degrading for the immigrants, but soon even these primitive camps were filled. Then we began to see vast tent cities where they stayed until more adequate housing could be provided. In the summer, living under canvas was dusty and the heat stifling; in the winter it was bitter cold, wet, and muddy. No one was happy with the arrangements, but the country simply did not have the means for anything better.

In the very beginning many newcomers were settled in abandoned buildings in such towns as Ramla, Jaffa, or Haifa, but—as these 1949 headlines show—such easy solutions soon ran out and new buildings and entire settlements had to be built.

| | |
|---|---|
| 7 March | 198 Settlements Planned for 1949 |
| 3 April | J.N.F. to Acquire Million Dunams |
| 27 April | Planned Austerity to Guide Mass Immigration |
| 3 May | 55 Settlements in 15 Months |
| 7 May | 55,960 in 24 Transit Camps |
| 27 May | Absorption Is Main Issue |

One of the most inspiring sights of those days was the transition from the transit camps with their waiting thousands, to the new settlements one saw on every side. Over the years the Jewish National Fund—JNF—had purchased great tracts of land from the contributions of Jews all over the world. Here this money was being used on a grand scale. Literally, from one day to another, we would see small groups of tiny houses where another group of immigrants were settling.

Around the cities we also began to see housing developments being built. These were mainly apartment building complexes and in 1949 over twenty-nine thousand family units were built. Today, as one drives about the country, one sees prosperous urban and agricultural settlements, but then most of the country was unsettled wilderness with relatively few settlements to be seen.

One day I happened to be riding in a taxi driven by a tourist guide who was taking some tourists down south to Beersheba. Suddenly, he exclaimed, "Good heavens, that settlement wasn't here last week." Later, I quietly asked if this was all part of the spiel for tourists and he indignantly insisted, "No, no, it really was not there." That's the way it really was. On every side we saw very modest beginnings spring up literally overnight and these would truly blossom into the country of today.

Then of course we had no way of knowing how all of these grand plans would develop, but today we see the results. Some years later I was taking a young foreman from a local factory home, and as we passed what had been the site of Shaar Aliyah he said, "That's where I first began to earn money." He went on to explain that he was just a small boy and he and his buddies would line the fence surrounding the camp and crowds of local residents looking for their relatives would pay these kids to look for the Rabinovitch family from Lodz, or the Ginsbergs from Zwikau.

As we arrived at his home he insisted that I come in to meet his wife. He proudly introduced me to his lovely wife and showed me the new baby. The flat was modest, but nicely furnished. He had a good job in a new factory and the transformation from a ragged kid in a mabarah occurred in but a very few years. Unfortunately, such permanent solutions took years, but people did settle down and build new lives.

There was a wave of all sorts of quick building schemes such as at Kiryat Shmona where the original housing was in aluminum sheet metal huts. This was the simplest sort of shantytown. Here, one saw thousands of these shining little one-room huts, and it was to be years before these disappeared and were replaced by apartment buildings.

Since a home even as basic as an aluminum hut was not enough, work had to be found so that new lives could be started. Hence, near every new settlement one would see gangs of men building roads. Today roads are built with heavy machinery, but this was long before Israel had such luxuries. These roads were built by hand. One would see men placing large stones onto what would be the roadway, and when these didn't fit they would bash them into shape with hammers. Primitive perhaps, but it was dignified work.

Another mass occupation was the planting of trees. In ancient days Israel was covered with forests, but these had long since disappeared so that much of the landscape was barren rocky hills. Many of today's forests were planted by these newcomers, but the tree-lined roads are of special interest.

During the fighting it was often found that convoys had no place in such a barren land to hide from aerial attack or observation. Hence, a special program of tree planting along the roads was inaugurated. At first these were very modest saplings. Today, however, the original object has virtually been forgotten, but one certainly sees lovely tree-lined roads all over the country.

As the overall picture developed, it was clear that the best solutions to housing and employment were long-term problems, but there was one basic problem that could not be pushed aside. How would we feed the population? Austerity was on its way, and this would be a period more difficult than anyone of us had known. It would take some time until real hardships would be felt, for this was a gradual process. As a starting point, however, let us see a bit of how Israelis dealt with their daily purchases in those early days.

Our daily shopping was done at a small grocery located down the street in a tiny wooden hut. There the grocer had large barrels and boxes of such staples as flour, rice, and sugar. Nothing was pre-packaged. He had an old set of scales and when you bought five hundred grams of sugar he would weigh this on the spot, often spilling sugar all over the place. Bags were of course nonexistent so one brought his own shopping bags to cart everything home. Eggs were carefully counted out into the customer's container, but soon we were using the powdered variety along with powdered milk.

Supermarkets and department stores were, of course, nonexistent. On the Mercaz, however, there were several more resplendent shops, but these too were tiny compared to American or European standards. The shopper would go from shop to shop to find what he needed. The fruit and vegetable shop might well have been simple open stalls. The American style drugstore was not to be found; the pharmacy was exactly that. There, one bought drugs, when available.

On every corner and sometimes in between, there was a kiosk or café where one could buy coffee, tea, soft drinks, and in the summer, ice cream. In the winter, ice cream disappeared from the market since everyone knew that in the cold weather one didn't eat ice cream.

Shopping for clothing was much the same as for food. The shops were tiny with a very limited selection. Despite this, however, the women managed to somehow or other keep up-to-date with the world's styles. Just before our leaving, the United States, the "New Look" appeared, which involved long skirts of mid-calf length.

In Israel, cloth along with everything else was in short supply, which made it a real problem for the women to appear with the New Look. However, the Israeli women were not to be left behind and they soon began to appear with all sorts of ingenious solutions to the long skirt.

Men's clothing was a much simpler matter. Khaki shorts, sport shirt, and knee socks were very common, and this was completely acceptable even for the manager of a bank. Evening wear for men consisted of slacks and a sport shirt, and dressed in this manner one could attend the most formal affair.

There was a very special spirit in the air, for the Jewish State existed and Herzl's dream of Jews returning from all over the world was a reality. Everyone was caught up in the whole concept of welcoming the newcomers and together rebuilding the country. We had no way of foreseeing the difficulties that lay ahead, but everyone felt a part of this pioneering effort. These difficulties would take their toll, but we all felt good to be a part of this historic effort.

# 20
# Spring 1949

Spring brought with it not only the yearly rebirth of nature, but a complete change in our lives. First, one must realize that in Israel the rains fall only in the winter, thus by the end of the hot summer the land, aside from irrigated patches, is brown. The winter rains start the growing cycle and with spring the countryside is literally blooming.

When driving through the countryside we saw beautiful fields of red poppies and yellow ragwort. Trees burst into bloom and in Haifa the wadis of Mount Carmel become a green jungle filled with wonderful wild flowers.

In those days the population on the Carmel was relatively small and picking wild flowers was a most popular and then innocent Shabat activity. Just a three minutes' walk from Bashir Street one could enter another world of green forest and wild flowers. We would usually return home with lovely bunches of poppies, cyclamens, and tiny little orchids. It was then that we learned the wonderful story of the cyclamens whose flowers droop instead of standing up straight.

It seems that these lovely purple flowers grew in the Garden of Eden, but in those days they stood up straight and proud. It seems, however, that when Eve ate the famous apple, they were so upset that they all hung their heads in shame. Thus they have remained ever since.

As the military political scene began to stabilize, the navy's activities became very routine and we began to think about the future. Those of us who had served as naval officers in World War II were of course always comparing the Israeli Navy with the American and British navies, which in a sense, was perhaps unfair; but certainly realistic.

Several new Americans had arrived with their families—Dick Rosenberg, Marvin Broder, and Sandy Finard—and each was an experienced naval officer. However, when one considers the entire navy it was obvious that we were desperately short of trained personnel, as well as the proper equipment with which to defend the country.

Since everything up to this time had been done literally on the spur of the moment, a small group of the volunteers suggested to Paul

Shulman, the navy's chief of staff, that we would like to outline our views on how we thought the navy of the future should be organized and present these to Yaacov Dori, then head of the armed forces.

Paul was very cooperative and agreed to arrange a meeting with Yaacov. In the meantime, David Delange, Alan Burke, Hal Notarius, and myself, spent considerable time preparing not only an appraisal of the navy's problems, but a suggested program on how the situation might be changed. On the big day, Jonny Leff and I started out for Tel Aviv and almost immediately we began to get insight into the military dilemma.

We were just a few miles outside of Haifa when we passed a tank carrier stuck beside the road. There was an armored car aboard and we stopped to see if we could be of any help. One of the soldiers explained in Canadian English that he was the driver of the armored car. Since it would be some time until the truck could be fixed, he asked if he could ride with us to Tel Aviv where he would meet up with the truck later.

The ride proved to be a revelation that the navy was not the only outfit in trouble. Our passenger had been in the Canadian Army's Armored Corp and like the rest of us, was a volunteer. The highlight of his dissertation on the army was when he exclaimed, "These people are crazy. They send me into battle with only seven shells. Now the security of the driver is really not very important, but can you imagine risking one of our only armored cars with only seven shells? Don't worry though, I've got an extra three that no one knows about. They're my reserve to get out of trouble if the need arises."

Yaacov Dori was very cooperative and listened attentively to our presentation, and then our education began. We began to discuss in general terms some of the points and then one of us started to justify something in our report. Whereupon, Dori interjected, "You don't have to justify anything. I agree wholeheartedly with everything you've said, but you don't understand my problem."

"I know what's wrong; I don't know what to do about it. We don't have proper equipment or money to buy it. We do not even know what we really need. On top of this we have no broad base of highly trained experts."

To make matters even more complex, he was also confronted with the problem that a large part of the armed forces was composed of foreigners. However, he rightly asked the question: "Can I really trust the armed services of the country to foreigners? Of course I respect these men and women who have volunteered their lives, but who are they and can I really be sure that they are not working for someone else?"

We were not completely happy about this last point, but looking back on this, he was completely correct. It was not too many years until we saw real evidence of such problems in the case of Israel Baer who rose to a very senior position in the army only to have it discovered that he was working for the Russians.

That day we learned that the problem was not nearly as simple as we had supposed, but one positive result of the meeting was the establishment of a planning commission to prepare detailed plans for the future.

As a result of this meeting a group of us were relieved of our commands and assigned to a planning board. We spent many weeks trying to come to grips with a reasonable master plan for the navy of the future.

Another interesting experience during this period was to attend an *ulpan*. Teaching Hebrew on a massive scale to the flood of immigrants was a problem that had been given a great deal of consideration. The ulpan was the approach that evolved. Actually, the word means "studio" and a Hebrew ulpan was a highly specialized intensified language course.

One of the problems that had to be faced was that the students usually spoke many different languages, and in many cases the teachers could not speak the student's language at all. Thus in principle the ulpan was a course in which only Hebrew was used and you learned by constant repetition.

The course to which I was sent was for volunteers in the army and there were young men and women from all over the world. We had classes all day long and most of the students actually lived at the school so the exposure was quite intensive. On the other hand, the course was only ten days, which is nowhere near the length of time required to learn the language.

The one advantage of this particular course was that the teachers and students were all young and full of spirit. Hence, no one was embarrassed to speak with mistakes. Every one did his best and laughed when the results were ludicrous.

At graduation time we all thought that we had really learned the language but, for someone as inept as I, this was just the beginning of many years' study. The ulpan did give us a feeling for the language, a basic vocabulary, and above all a lack of inhibitions about speaking. Right or wrong, you said it.

The one thing the ulpan could not change was the accent and for the so-called "Anglo-Saxons," the accent is like wearing a label. On many occasions I would explain something in Hebrew with a carefully rehearsed speech only to be told, "I'm sorry, I don't speak English."

Then I would repeat another little speech about how I was not speaking English. Even today if I answer the phone with one word, *hello*, the caller may well exclaim, "Oh, you speak English."

On the home front we were also making progress. Davy was now in nursery school, which was the norm in Israel. There he quickly learned the Hebrew of a young man of almost two. The important thing is that he felt at home and was quite at ease in his new environment. A natural corollary of the language was the music of little people, and we all began to learn Hebrew nursery rhymes and songs of all the holidays.

It never fails to amaze me how quickly little people learn new languages, apparently without the slightest difficulty. One day Davy returned from play and told us how he had had a long conversation with one of the neighbors. It all made sense until we realized that the woman did not speak English or Hebrew so we asked Davy how he had talked to her. His reply was quite simple, "In Yiddish"—a language he certainly hadn't heard at home.

Unfortunately, his linguistic endeavors were not always so cute, for one day we heard him shouting a catchy phrase in Arabic. We were quite proud that he was learning Israel's second language. That evening we visited very good friends and proudly mentioned that Davy was beginning to speak Arabic. With knowing grins everyone asked what he had said. When we replied there were gales of laughter and finally someone explained that he was shouting, "Eat shit."

Of course everyone thought this was very funny and word naturally got around the neighborhood. For a time we were quite concerned whenever we heard him shouting something we didn't understand, and a week or so later another incident occurred. He was shouting something and, taking no chances, I ran down the stairs past Alex Kolsky who was standing in his doorway. As I went past he hollered to me, "It's OK, he's just saying, 'Come here'." Without being told, Alex knew exactly what was on my mind.

One incident that perhaps exemplifies how much at ease the youngsters felt, comes to mind. As health hazards arose, there were programs of mass inoculation of whatever was the latest fashion. One afternoon we found ourselves in line with Davy to receive some sort of shot that to an adult might not have been so serious, but to a very little boy it was very frightening.

Davy was apprehensive but reasonably confident until it came to his turn and then he couldn't contain himself and burst into tears. The nurse dressed in her street clothes covered with a white smock saw this crying child and suddenly took him in her arms and began to comfort him in Yiddish. Davy certainly did not understand the words, but the obvious intent gave him confidence.

Of course,the shot was over in a moment and we were on our way, but the incident was typical of the time and even of today. A stranger is often introduced or referred to as aunt or uncle, which meant that every older person was somehow related. To the little people this was a very comforting thing.

Davy, in his *gan*—kindergarten—had many buddies, and by this time Daddy and Mommie also had theirs. There was a very active social life of the newcomers to Haifa and the old-timers were most gracious in absorbing us in their midst. A particularly nice development was the Friday night dinners that became a custom at Four Bashir Street.

Dinner on Friday night is of course a special occasion to welcome the Sabbath, and usually families spend the evening together. However, none of us at Four Bashir had families nearby so we began to have Friday night dinners together. Each Friday we met at someone else's house and in a sense we were one large family. To be sure, everyone had a very different background, but there was one unifying factor: we were all Jews. Moreover, we were sharing the same Israeli experience.

With the change of season our political outlook also began to change. The war seemed to be over despite the fact that there were no peace treaties, and our thinking began to turn to civilian activities. The interesting stories of the day began to include such topics as the building of new agricultural settlements, reforestation projects, and new homes for immigrants. Employment for the newcomers was also a fundamental need, which meant that industries had to be built. This latter activity seemed to be most attractive to me and I soon found myself ready to become a civilian again.

# 21
# Getting Started in Industry

That spring there were many signs that the war had more or less ended and that the country's priorities were shifting from defense to building an economy that could support the huge influx of immigrants. All sorts of changes were taking place.

One particular change occurred right under our noses in Haifa. Until this time the number of vehicles on the road was minimal and problems of traffic control were literally nonexistent. However, in Haifa there seemed to be some problems brewing, so the municipality decided on a daring project. They would install Israel's first traffic light.

In a sense this really was a daring project, for in a country completely devoid of traffic lights, how would drivers, who had never seen such a thing, know what to do when they came to a red light. The solution was very ingenious. At the busiest corner in Haifa the new light was installed, and on its first day there were also policemen to instruct drivers on how to behave.

One policeman stood under the light and directed traffic according to the light above. There was also a policeman on each corner to tell every driver what to do as he approached the intersection. One friend who went through this indoctrination had an interesting story to tell, which truly foretold the future of Israeli driving habits.

Being an American, she knew all about traffic lights, so when the light turned amber she slowed down. However, the policeman at her corner frantically motioned her to speed up. Somewhat mystified, she ignored the policeman's signals and stopped. Whereupon he came over to the car and said: "Don't you understand how traffic lights work? When it's green you go, when it's red you stop, and when it's amber you go like hell to get across before it turns red."

More concrete signs of progress were also seen along the roads in the country. On every side we saw new settlements, but the one view I particularly enjoyed was of a large field near Herzlia filled with huge earth-moving machinery—all part of an American aid program. Before this time bulldozers, tractors, and earth-moving machinery in Israel were small, few, and far between. However, this grand display of modern equipment would soon change the entire character of public works and agriculture. Handmade roads would soon be a thing of the past.

Vic and I both saw our futures in industry rather than the army, and when Vic suggested that we set up an engineering consulting firm, this sounded like just the right approach. Leaving the army took less time than it takes to write about it since there were no organized procedures.

It took about a year for the administration to catch up with me. For some strange reason Shlomo Shamir, who had become chief of staff for the navy, felt that we had to set the record straight. It was only then that I went to the induction center near Tel Aviv and in the course of a morning was formally inducted and discharged, according to the proper dates. Israeli bureaucracy was beginning to take hold.

Avrunin and Gershoni, Engineers, became a reality, and one of our first proejcts was to contact every prospective client in the country. Since we were to find that there were very few suitable candidates, this was far easier than it might sound. There was a *Red Book*, which listed every Israeli firm; thus we were able to send letters to every industrial plant in the country. Later we followed up on the letters with phone calls and then plant visits.

Some months later the Palestine Economic Corporation asked me to make a detailed survey of the Haifa Bay industrial area, and this complemented our countrywide survey. These two surveys were actually separated by some months, but to make it easier for the reader, I'll merge the results of both into one description.

It should be noted here that Haifa Bay was to be the Detroit of Israel. The main and only real port of the country was in Haifa and surrounding Haifa Bay was a large flat plain ideal for heavy industry. There were some well-known factories in the Bay area and the Palestine Economic Corporation was anxious to get a detailed picture of what was really out there.

There were indeed about a dozen fair-sized plants in the Bay area (factories employing several hundred workers). The railroad workshop was truly a large machine shop devoted to keeping the railroad in repair. The refinery was also in the big leagues, but since the flow of petroleum had been stopped by the surrounding Arab states, its production was quite limited.

Vulcan Foundries, Phonecia Glass Works, and Atta Textiles were also large well-established firms in the Bay area, but this about ended the list of big factories. I also found around a dozen large workshops in the area that employed ten to twenty workers. The remainder of the Middle East's answer to Detroit consisted of about twenty small workshops employing anywhere from one to ten workers. These produced all sorts of products ranging from chocolates to battery acid for automobiles.

This latter plant was perhaps most characteristic of these small enterprises. Pure sulfuric acid for car batteries was in short supply and an enterprising chemist built a "plant" to fill the need. The entire office and factory occupied a space roughly the size of a large bathroom.

There I saw two glass laboratory stills in which crude sulfuric acid produced by the refinery could be purified for use in batteries. On the one hand the whole operation could not even be called a laboratory; on the other hand, this "plant" did supply the local requirements.

All sorts of important needs were satisfied by such enterprising immigrants with special skills. Similarly, a friend, who was also a chemist, supplied the needs of pharmaceutical laboratories for pure caffeine. He had arranged with a number of cafés to save their coffee grounds, which he periodically collected. Then in a bathroom lab at home he extracted the remaining caffeine.

One of my most pleasant visits in the Haifa Bay area was to one of the country's leading chocolate factories. This was located in an old Arab style residence. It was a rabbit warren of tiny vaulted rooms connected by Byzantine arches. Each small compartment contained some sort of makeshift ancient machine churning out candies.

The owner was very proud of his products and at each machine he insisted that I taste the latest delicacy. What he was doing with such primitive facilities was quite remarkable and I must have gained several kilos during a most enjoyable visit.

Another example that has always stuck in my mind was the sheet metal "factory" that manufactured small boats for use in the budding fish pond industry of the kibbutzim. The owner, and only worker, proudly showed me several boats, that he had made, but the fascinating thing about the entire operation was his source of raw material.

When I asked where he was able to get sheet metal he explained that the government gave virtually no import licenses for raw materials, so he had found his own source.

There were at that time a great abundance of old fifty-five-gallon oil drums that were virtually valueless. Our entrepreneur would buy up the old drums, painstakingly take these apart, and then he rerolled the metal to remove the ridges and straighten the sheet. From the salvaged drums he made his boats.

This was typical of the situation at that time. The government had practically no foreign currency with which to operate. Defense, immigration, and food came first. Thus, there was virtually nothing left over for industrial raw materials.

In essence these few plants epitomize the industry in the Bay area. Yes, there were a few proper factories, but the vast infrastructure needed to build and support real industry simply did not exist. Unfortunately, the rest of the country's "industry" was much the same. We saw carpentrys, concrete block plants, machine shops, tile plants, and all sorts of small outfits; however, few were more than little workshops.

As Vic and I toured the country we saw many examples of ingenuity and grim determination. One such plant noted in the *Red Book* was a "uniform factory." All four workers sat at their sewing machines pedaling away, since none of the machines were motorized. When someone ran out of work you would hear him holler, "Hey Shmullick." Then Shmullick would pick up any ready pieces at his machine and toss these over the heads of the others to the man needing work.

When I asked about specialized machinery such as a button-hole machine or a button sewer, they mentioned that neighbors had some of these machines and worked as subcontractors. This was the way a garment factory functioned in my grandfather's time, but certainly not in 1949.

One should not be misled by the fact that so many "plants" were tiny, for all sorts of important work was done in these workshops. Many immigrants to the country were craftsmen and had either brought with them or somehow acquired one or two basic machines. In literally every hole in the wall one found such "factories." The cities of Tel Aviv and Haifa had whole areas that were literally catacombs of these tiny workshops.

Much of the work was done in the streets or in open courtyards. Occasionally one would be surprised to find that several adjacent areas had been joined together into what might have been called a little factory. For many years, if one needed any particular service one had to prowl around the catacombs until the right expert was found.

The problems were not just associated with locating the right expert, for all manner of parts, tools, hardware and supplies simply were not available. Importing such necessary items was impossible, and so all sorts of primitive expedients were employed.

These craftsmen did their best, but one would often see very strange results. A cabinetmaker would show you a beautiful piece of furniture with the most bizarre handles. Or one would see a very ingenious piece of handmade machinery with outlandish makeshift switches or valves. Of course they knew better; they did the best they could with what they had.

Against this dismal background there were signs of an awakening. One of our clients was a group of foreign investors who were building a large pipe mill near Tel Aviv. Our job was to lay out the plant and help ease their way in terms of solving local problems.

Another large project concerned the purchase of thousands of Quonset huts from a U.S. steel manufacturer, to be used as immigrant housing. There was enormous pressure on the government to supply the flood of immigrants with some form of housing and Quonset huts were a rather nice solution to the problem.

We arranged to have one of these huts assembled and furnished right on the grounds of the Housing Ministry in Tel Aviv-Hakirya. There were all sorts of complaints about the strange shape, but the advantages of price and quick delivery far outweighed the objections. Thus the decision was made to go ahead with the project and we looked forward to a very busy future.

Unfortunately, it was not to be. A few weeks later there was a national steel strike in the United States, and when our supplier could not make delivery, as per the contract, the whole project collapsed. These were indeed difficult times.

The papers told about new industrial centers being planned at Acre and Netanya, so we went out to see what was going on. In each case we had the same experience. First, we sat with the city planners and heard wonderful stories of the industry that would support the city's population. Then, we would ask: "When is this all going to happen?"

In both cities our hosts said, "Come and see." To our amazement, in each city there were large areas being leveled, roads under construction, and buildings being erected. It would take years for these areas to really develop, but the start was being made.

Perhaps the best summary of the situation is in the story about the head of the Nur match factory. His matches were famous for all the wrong reasons. A good percentage of these would not light. The major complaint, however, was that in many cases the match would light, but the flaming head would fly off the stick and land on someone's clothing. Thus one day a letter to the *Palestine Post* suggested that the man responsible for such destruction and waste should be prosecuted.

In the short space allotted for rebuttal, however, the owner of the factory presented a completely different point of view. He claimed that it was quite a feat to be able to produce any matches at all. He had built his machinery from junk, and had to make do with all sorts of substitute raw materials. Then, as if adding insult to injury, he had to manufacture the matches with completely untrained help.

In his eyes the community should have given him a medal. Some months later when I became a factory manager I began to see that his remarks were completely justified.

Thus it was after the war of liberation that Israel's industrial resources were minimal, but everywhere you saw a certain optimistic dynamism. People were active building a country. It would take years for the results to be felt, but today we see that these stumbling attempts did build an industrial economy.

## 22
# We Meet the Habibis

Living as we were, in a country at war, our daily contacts were mainly with the Jewish community, it was only rarely that we met the Arabs. However, with time, such contacts became more frequent. During the previous winter I was notified by headquarters that I was invited to a cocktail party to be given by Victor Hayat, one of the wealthy Arabs of Haifa. Being very new in the community I really had no idea what this was all about, but was told that this was a gesture of conciliation.

The party was held at the home of the host in an area, which to this day, is a "mixed neighborhood." As one might expect, the place was packed and since it had been a long hard day I was mainly interested in finding a seat. As I circulated through the distinguished crowd of visitors, I spotted a beautiful ottomon that was apparently vacant. It seemed to be a large round footstool with a beautiful brass base. Just the place to rest my weary bones.

It took a minute or two to worm my way across the room, but I finally made it. I couldn't understand why no one else was taking advantage of what appeared to be the only vacant seat in the room, but then it all became clear. I was just about to sit down when, to my horror, I felt waves of heat radiating from this seat. Only then I realized that what I had thought to be an ottoman was in reality a charcoal brazier used to heat the room. It was truly elegant, but hardly a place to sit.

A moment later I felt someone grab my arm and our good friend Jacob Solomon began pulling me across the room saying, "There's someone I want you to meet." Before I knew what was happening, he brought me to a rather distinguished-looking man who obviously was a foreigner—he was wearing a suit with a necktie. Jacob exuberantly exclaimed to the gentleman, "I want you to meet one of your boys whose doing a wonderful job."

However, before we could shake hands, Jacob's wife, Sarah, muttered something to Jacob and dragged me away. I was completely bewildered until Sarah explained. The gentlemen was the American consul and she was sure that he was the last one I wanted to meet.

128

Some months later the whole family received a similar invitation, this time to lunch in the city of Acre. This was to be quite a special occasion, for in those days Acre consisted of only the ancient walled city and was populated solely by Arabs. The town had been captured by the Israeli Army very early in the war, and, since there was heavy fighting in the area, it was decided to close the city.

This meant that the local population lived their normal lives within the city. However, they could not leave and had no communication with the outside world until the fighting subsided. Efforts were made to ease the residents' needs and among other things, there was a Christian mission that had a special educational program. The military governor of the city was Rehavam Amir, who happened to be our upstairs neighbor.

Rehavam and Avital were very close friends and it was Rehavam who asked if we would like to join him as guests at a conciliatory get-together in Acre. In this case, the owner of Abbu Christo, a lovely restaurant on Acre Bay, had invited Rehavam and specifically requested that he bring other guests. We were, of course, pleased to join the party and on the following Shabbat we set out for Acre. It was on the way that Rehavam explained one very important rule of the game. "Whatever they serve, you eat."

We were very cordially received and in due course the meal began with the traditional plates of *humus* and *thina*. All innocent enough, but since arriving in the country I had done my best to avoid these dishes. For some stupid reason these very common Middle Eastern dishes simply did not seem like they were the sort of things I wanted to eat. Now, however, according to Rehavam's warning, I had little choice. So with great trepidation I tore off a piece of *pitta*, dipped into the humus and very cautiously tasted this omnious dish only to find that it was really delicious.

Rehavam was a very special person and in a sense famous, but we were not to learn of this for almost a year. He was born in Poland and lived there until the age of seventeen. It was then that his parents decided that he simply could not remain in Poland and sent him to live with his grandfather in Jerusalem.

As Rehavam once explained, he had lived in terror of guns as a boy and could not be persuaded to even touch one; however, after reaching Jerusalem guns took on another meaning entirely. It was not very long before he joined the Palmach, which in those days, was the elite force of the Jewish settlers. We were close friends of the Amirs, but this was about all we knew of Rehavam's past. It took almost a year before we heard the interesting parts.

One evening Rehavam and Avital were entertaining an American guest and we were invited to join the party. It seems that the guest of honor was quite taken with the story of how the British had recruited Jews from Palestine with European backgrounds and parachuted them into Eastern Europe as undercover agents. He seemed to be fascinated by the exploits of Reuven Dafne who was one of these famous agents. Finally, however, Avital's aunt couldn't stand it any longer and blurted out, "Our Rehavam was not only one such agent, but he was parachuted behind the German lines twice."

It was interesting to realize that we had been good friends for almost a year before we learned this. He was simply too modest to mention it. Afterward, however, we did talk of such things and one particular incident concerning Acre has always stuck in my mind.

Military information was somehow being leaked from the city of Acre, which seemed like an impossibility since the city was sealed. This bothered Rehavam's professional sense and he gave a lot of thought to just how this could be happening. Then one day he came to a most disagreeable conclusion. The source of the leak could only be the head of the Christian mission who had free access to come and go as he pleased.

Thus in the true tradition of his previous life, as a secret agent, he let slip a completely fictitious plan that would invoke great hardship on the local Arab residents. He was most careful to repeat this story to only one person, and then he sat back and waited. Sure enough, two days later an Arab delegate at the United Nations in New York made a formal protest about this dastardly plan and insisted that the United Nations take action to prevent it.

I never knew just how serious these leaks actually were and what happened, but the incident is the sort that hangs about the back of one's mind.

Up until this time our personal contacts with Arabs were more or less nonexistent. One of the women's favorite hairdressers in Haifa was Avram, an Arab in partnership with a Jew, but that was the extent of such contact for us. However, one day our isolation was penetrated.

It was during the summer of 1949 that we first met our landlady and that precipitated a number of experiences that added to our understanding of the country.

Number Four Bashir Street was one of a number of buildings owned by well-to-do Arabs, which had been rented to British officials during the Mandate. When the British left, many flats were empty, and it was found that the owners had also left the country. Since there was a desperate shortage of apartments, any unattended building was an invitation to the homeless to simply move in and take over.

In order to control this situation, the government set up a special office, the Custodian of Abandoned Property, which acted as a surrogate landlord. We had originally been billeted in our flat by the navy but when the custodian's office took over the property, we signed a proper lease and paid rent to the custodian. The custodian, in turn, looked after the building and kept the proceeds for the owner until he returned.

Then one evening the doorbell rang and we found an Arab woman dressed in black at the door. She explained in excellent English that she was Mrs. Habibi and that she owned the building. We, of course, invited her in and she told us that at the beginning of the war, her husband had left the country with two of their children, leaving her with the rest of her family in Haifa. Since the property was in the name of her husband, it had been classified as abandoned property and had been taken over by the custodian.

However, Mr. Habibi had died in Lebanon and his property had been willed to his widow. Since Mrs. Habibi, the legal owner, lived in the country, she requested that the custodian return her property and within a short period this was done. From then on we paid our rent directly to her, and over the years we had a very pleasant relationship.

At that time Mrs. Habibi was living in a tiny room in one of the Christian churches together with her other children. This, of course, was a temporary solution to her housing problem. Since she suddenly became owner of a great deal of property she decided to build an extra story to one of her buildings in Haifa.

There was one very serious problem, however, obtaining the necessary building materials. There were actually two sources. One could apply to the government for a license to buy materials at the controlled prices. However, such licenses were extremely difficult to obtain. On the other hand one could buy on the black market, but there the prices were prohibitive. In her case, however, she made application for a license and to our surprise she received it in a very short time.

Then in the fall we had another visitor, George Habibi—Mrs. Habibi's son. George was one of the children taken to the Lebanon with Mr. Habibi and he had been studying at the American University in Beirut. George was a very pleasant fellow. He was short, heavyset, had a ready smile, spoke excellent English, and loved to drop in and visit.

After his father's death he and his sister had found themselves alone in Lebanon, separated from their mother and from the rest of the family. There were quite a few cases of such broken families and as peace seemed to be drawing near, the government had allowed the reunification of families. Thus, George and his sister had come home to Haifa.

On his first visit he had a special problem. George had finished his first year at the American University in Beirut and wanted to continue at the Technion in Haifa—then Israel's only engineering school. He had applied, but was very concerned that he would not be accepted because he was an Arab. Thus he had turned to the tenants of Four Bashir Street. Would we help him?

To my amazement the neighbors said that they would be glad to arrange things for George. This was particularly surprising to me since every day we read in the papers that the Arabs had every intention of throwing us into the sea. Moreover, almost daily we would read about acts of terrorism or violence, so these threats were something to be taken seriously. Thus I asked how we could help such youngsters? In essence, we would be educating him to push us into the sea.

It was then that I was put in my place. "You don't understand the government's policy of peaceful coexistence with Israel's Arabs," they explained. "Youngsters like George obviously must continue their education. We can't expect such a boy to be satisfied with some menial job. Thus he has to have an education and it's our duty to help him."

Sure enough, George was back in a few weeks later to tell me the good news; he had been accepted and was going to study civil engineering.

Since George had always talked English even to the neighbors, I asked him one evening if he spoke Hebrew. He said no, but by the time studies started he thought he would be quite fluent since Arabic and Hebrew are somewhat similar. It seemed so unfair that he could pick up the language in but a few months whereas it would take me many years.

Several years later George did receive his degree in civil engineering and then decided that he would like to get a master's degree in the United States. In one of our talks he mentioned that Israel was not the place for him and that his real intention was to settle in the United States and then bring his family over there.

At the time, due to the shortage of foreign currency, there was considerable competition among the youngsters who wanted to continue their education abroad. However, it was not long before George did get the necessary allotment of dollars and was off to the United States.

Many years later I met one of Israel's diplomats who had been the Israeli cultural attaché in New York at that time and by chance the name George Habibi came up. I was then able to hear the next chapter in this particular story.

George received his master's degree, but he found that the United States was not really what he had expected. He then decided that maybe Israel really was the place for him. He returned and set up his own contracting business and I was always pleased to see signs on buildings under construction advertising that the builder was George Habibi.

It is important to realize at this point that one might hear all sorts of stories about relations with the Arab community, but in this personal account I can only report the way it was—for me.

# 23
# Israel, the Land of Dreams

The summer and fall of 1949 were exciting in that all sorts of wonderful things were happening. Every day we read about developments that would make our dream of a modern country come true.

| | |
|---|---|
| 1 June | Myerson Plan to Build 30,000 Houses in 5 Months |
| 2 June | Million More Dunams Being Farmed |
| 23 June | 130,000 Came in 5 Months |
| 24 June | Half-Million Sapling Orchards to Be Planted |
| 4 July | Israel Reaches Million Mark |
| 24 July | IP200 Million [about $300 million] Invested in Past 6 Months |
| 2 September | 214,000 Immigrants Accommodated Outside Camps |

The country was beginning to cope with the enormous problem of accomodating the flood of immigrants. Houses were being built, land settled, orchards planted, and investments were made in industry.

Each of these headlines referred to enormous projects that were developing all around us, and we felt a part of this wave of progress. I couldn't help but remember how the great United States found it extremely difficult to accept one hundred thousand DPs and the rest of the developed world were unable to absorb any at all. However, here in our little speck on the map of the world, Israel, an infant nation with only a million people, we were not only accepting every Jew who wanted to come, but were also building homes and an economy to support them.

In 1949 we were a country of dreamers planning all sorts of large enterprises such as:

| | |
|---|---|
| 27 June | Israeli Vessels Will Ply Between Haifa-NY |

134

| | |
|---|---|
| 13 September | New Fertilizer Plant Opened |
| 16 October | Sunflower Oil Experiment |
| 1 November | Refineries Working Again |
| 3 November | Milk Will Flow in Israel Soon<br>3,000 American Cows Imported |
| 9 November | 2 New Plants Solel Boneh<br>Electric Motors and Steel Pipes |

Such stories preluded enormous strides for the new country, but each plant had a long hard row to hoe. It would take many years before these dreams would actually materialize. For example, one day while in Tel Aviv, I bumped into Danny Schind. Danny had been one of the Israelis whom I had met while working for the Jewish Agency in New York. He had started out buying ships for smuggling illegal immigrants, and with the coming of the new State of Israel, had become head of the Shoham Shipping Company.

We dropped into one of the seaside cafés for a cup of coffee where Danny told me all about the two liberty ships he had just bought. These were part of a large project to make Israel independent of foreign shipping companies. According to the plan, it was hoped that within three to four years most cargoes would travel in Israeli ships, and that all Israeli ships would be manned by Israeli crews.

However, as with the rest of the country's dreams, this was not so simple. I can still hear Danny's sigh as he moaned: "Where will I find Jewish sailors?" Buying ships was only a small part of the problem; the real issue was to man the ships with competent Israeli crews and this could not be done overnight. The solution was to set up a nautical school to train merchant marine officers in Acre and over a period of years Israeli crews were trained for Danny's new ships, but not overnight as he would have liked.

It seemed a strange idea, at the time, to extract edible oil from sunflower seeds, but today this is commonplace. Along the Haifa–Tel Aviv road today, after thirty-five years, one sees huge fields of lovely sunflowers. In the supermarkets sunflower cooking oil and cholesterol-free margarine are taken for granted.

The fact that the refineries were again in operation was truly of great importance, for our Arab neighbors had cut all the pipelines and refused to supply the necessary crude oil. However, alternate sources were found and the oil was now coming to the refinery in ships and Israel had a source of fuel.

However, this too was not quite so easy and on 23 December we would see headlines about how the refinery had to shut down due to insufficient oil. It would be years until a stable source of fuel would be supplied and the refineries could operate normally.

Solel Boneh was a large industrial company owned by the Histadrut—the labor union—and the announcement of their pipe plant had an interesting sidelight. The article explained how the pipe mill supplying the necessary pipes for new settlements and agriculture would be completed in a year.

Actually it was not started for a year and little did I suspect that I would build this factory.

Most of the headlines in those months of 1949, however, referred to more modest developments, more in keeping with the struggling ministate.

| | |
|---|---|
| 12 August | New Garbage Trucks for Jerusualem |
| 15 August | Export Market for Ice-Boxes |
| 30 September | Phone Calls to Europe |
| 2 October | Drivers Beware<br>Police Cars Now Have Radios |
| 8 November | Silk Screen Printing Plant |

Such stories more accurately depicted the true state of affairs. The story of Jerusalem's new garbage trucks concerned the acquisition of five new vehicles. In the United States not very important, but to the struggling community this was a sign of progress that one could actually see on the streets.

Who would actually think of exporting ice-boxes even in those days? However, when one thinks about the fact that very few Israelis had refrigerators and that there were other countries in the same boat, this little plant filled a need, if only a temporary one.

Phone calls to Europe—so what? First of all, virtually no one had a phone in those days. Thus if you were lucky enough to have one, who could you call? Second, the overseas lines went through Arab countries and had long since been severed. We were cut off from the outside world.

It would be years before proper undersea cables would be laid and real communication restored. However, this expedient of a radio telephone link to Europe was better than nothing. Well, not very much better. On some family occasions we did get calls from the United

States via the radio link and our neighbor's phone. We really didn't hear very much and had to scream to be heard, but one always felt good having talked to the family in the States.

The majority of the new plants were more like the silk screen printing plant that employed two workers. These wonderful headlines did tell about progress, but we did not realize that building a modern economy is like building a house. One needs to assemble a lot of little bricks. Each by itself is not too significant. However, each has its own contribution and together they form the overall structure.

Vic and I were plodding along in our consulting business, but it seemed that most people were completely absorbed with the birth of their dream factories and had little time with such mundane problems as feasibility and productivity.

One approach we used was to talk with importers to see the sort of products that might be made locally and in one such meeting I began to see Israel through the eyes of a British exporter and perhaps through the eyes of all outsiders.

It was suggested that I look through a book of correspondence in which various British firms offered their products. One of the first letters suggested an interesting idea. Since they did not have an office in Israel, they suggested that we deal directly with their office in Beirut.

It seemed strange that a cosmopolitan firm exporting products all over the world would be unaware of the fact that we were still officially at war with Lebanon and thus had no contact with their representative in Beirut.

Another letter contributing to my education was from a farming tool manufacturer who offered an implement that might be of use to "the natives in the hill country."

British firms were still quite well entrenched in Israel and we often saw large ads of Imperial Chemical Industries, which led to a rather humorous exchange. In one of these ads they mentioned an extensive line of resins for laminates. Since Vic and I had been interested in laminates for armor plating, it seemed like a good idea to contact them.

The manager of the office was English with a very proper British accent. When I explained with my very American accent that I was interested in resins for laminates, he immediately explained that Imperial Chemical Industries did not produce such materials. He couldn't understand why one would put resins in such a product. I in turn explained that resins were basic to the production of laminates and couldn't understand why he was unaware of the fact, since his firm had advertised that they had such resins for sale.

We didn't seem to be getting anywhere so I turned to leave and he suddenly said, "Wait a moment. How do you spell it?" I then said resins for *l-a-m-i-n-a-t-e-s* he burst out laughing, and explained that he thought I wanted to use resins in lemonade.

It seemed that on the one hand we had all sorts of illusions of the great progress Zionists had made reclaiming the desert, but in reality, the country was an infant attempting to recover from its birth. In 1949 very little industrial development had actually taken place. For the entire year Israel only exported 1P10,600,000 (about $16,500,000); of this, 60 percent was citrus fruit and another 17 percent was polished diamonds. Thus Israel had really not entered the industrial export market.

This very low rate of industrial activity, of course, had its effect on our consulting business. Vic and I soon found that, although here and there we were able to find useful projects, there simply was not enough work to support two families. The only solution was to split up, and in my case, to find a job.

To finance this transition it was necessary to sell our Dodge and we began to live like normal Israelis riding the buses. This was quite an experience. The service was good, but the buses were antiquated rickety homemade affairs. The front doors were closed by springs that could be forced open from outside. Thus one would occasionally see some adventuresome soul running madly after a bus that had just left the bus stop, jump on the step, and while the bus was careening down the street, he would pry open the door and slip into the bus.

It seems that one day a middle-aged man accomplished this feat and on entering the bus a woman passenger said, "You're crazy to do such a thing; you ought to be in Blumenthal's," the local insane asylum. To this the man replied, "Madam, I am Blumenthal."

It was not long before I met Alexander ("Sasha") Goldberg and received an offer that was hard to refuse. Sasha was head of a new firm, Fertilizers and Chemicals, which had recently been opened and manufactured superphosphate fertilizers. However, Sasha had his own very extravagant dream for the firm. He was going to produce nitrates and build a heavy chemical industry.

At our first meeting I found him to be a very likable person and in all the years I was to know him I never changed this view. He was a short, round, middle-aged man with a pleasant smile and manner. When he began to tell me his plans for the future, he glowed. His accent was strictly British, but at the drop of a hat he could switch to Russian or Hebrew.

Sasha had been a member of a large and successful consulting firm in England and was involved in all sorts of industrial projects ranging from munitions to artificial limbs. He was a doer and nothing seemed to slow him down.

Before one of his trips to England he had been told that we had two hundred veterans needing artificial limbs so he walked into the largest prostheses manufacturer in England and announced that he wanted two hundred assorted arms and legs. The president of the firm was quite shocked, but patiently explained that it didn't work that way. Each patient had to be fitted with a custom-made appliance.

This didn't bother Sasha at all. He bought the equipment to build such a plant in Israel and brought several experts along to teach the Israeli staff.

At our first meeting he explained that in order for the country's agriculture to expand, it was vital that we produce three basic fertilizers: potash, phosphates, and nitrates. Since potash was extracted from the Dead Sea and phosphates were now being produced by Fertilizers and Chemicals, there remained only the nitrates. Nitrates, however, were an enormous problem, for these required a very substantial industrial complex; this was Sasha's dream.

Would I care to be his assistant? The sheer size and scope of the operation were irresistible. Moreover, what I couldn't realize at that time was that Sasha and I would become very close friends.

# 24
# Fertilizers and Chemicals Ltd.

During the winter of 1949–50 Israel was all of one and a half years old, and faced enormous problems. We were still threatened by war, involved in endless diplomatic negotiations, the enormous influx of new immigrants continued, over ninety thousand people were living in tents without employment, and we had virtually no facilities to cope.

Small factories were being set up and these went relatively quickly. However, we were beginning to realize that instant industries were not possible. The large enterprises we so desperately needed, were mostly in the planning stage, and Fertilizers and Chemicals is a good example of just what this implied.

Our site was located in the middle of the largely unoccupied plane surrounding Haifa Bay far from the main road. Since this was the wettest winter in recorded history, and the area was subject to flooding, the little cluster of buildings often looked like an island in the middle of a huge lake.

Few people had cars and there was no public transport to the factory, so early each morning a truck would meet the Haifa workers at Haifa's Armon Theater, to bring us to work. Similarly at night the truck would take us back to Haifa. If you missed the truck in either direction a taxi was the only solution.

These trucks had large, locally made, wooden bodies and were essentially for hauling industrial materials. However, since twice a day they had to transport passengers they were equipped with simple folding benches and canvas tops.

It was on my first day that I solved a problem that had often puzzled me. It seemed that Israel had been inundated with lawyers. Everywhere one saw men with leather briefcases so often carried by lawyers in the United States. The fact that they may have been lawyers in Europe before the war was understandable, but what did so many lawyers do in Israel?

On the bus to the plant my first day I found that most of my new colleagues were such briefcase lawyers. Then around noon it all be-

140

came clear. Out of the briefcases came sandwiches and thermos bottles, but the story did not end there. After work everyone stopped at the greengrocers to see if anything special was available, and again the briefcase came into its own.

"Potatoes! Wonderful, I'll have two kilos." The ever ready briefcase would be opened and in would go two kilos of potatoes fresh out of the ground. What else could one do? Bags and wrapping paper were unknown. In some of the better shops, for special customers, the proprietor would wrap one's purchase in a piece of yesterday's newspaper. The interesting thing was that it never occurred to anyone that it should be otherwise.

The site itself was quite empty, for the small sulfuric acid plant and the superphosphate plant occupied two relatively small sheds. The rest of the plant consisted of some storage buildings, a workshop, and offices. The offices were small one-story concrete block buildings with corrugated iron roofs. It was all right out of a book on pioneering in Israel.

The technical staff was also very small, for we were not going to design the various facilities. Today such factories would be designed in Israel, but in 1950 we simply did not have the expertise and experience. Thus the several plants that would comprise the new works would be designed and supplied by contractors in Europe and the United States.

Sasha had already been working with a number of foreign firms who were preparing their bids for the new plants. My job was to coordinate these proposals, attempt to resolve local problems, and then produce an overall plan complete with the required budget.

One very revealing problem that occurred in the very early stages of the planning concerned the type of sulfuric acid plant that would be needed for the new products. Sulfuric acid is one of the most basic industrial materials and one often can use the sulfuric acid output of a country to estimate its industrial development. It seems that there is no end to the uses of this material.

The acid plant needed for the superphosphates was microscopic and produced perhaps ten tons per day. The only other plant in Israel was at the refineries where they produced only enough for their own use. Thus again we can see that our efforts to build an industrial society were just beginning.

Our problem at that time was to select the process for the new plant that would produce forty tons of acid each day. To us this "large" output seemed like an enormous stride forward. Sulfur was the most logical raw material, but unfortunately Israel had no sulfur, thus it would have to be imported from the United States. On the other hand, there seemed to be a very attractive alternative process using gypsum, which Israel has in abundance.

The whole problem centered around the fact that the minimum-size plant for the gypsum process produced 100 tons of acid per day, and what would we do with the extra 60 tons of acids each day? It simply never occurred to anyone that this "huge" over capacity could be absorbed by the economy, so we finally settled for the conventional sulfur plant. Today, Fertilizers and Chemicals Ltd. makes 600 tons per day and is only one of several producers.

Another revealing problem, which had all sorts of interesting ramifications, concerned the soil on our site. The machinery envisaged for the new plants was to be large and very heavy, which meant massive foundations. However, we were blessed with a peculiar type of soil not very well suited to supporting great loads. Thus, one of our first problems was to find a geologist to give us some professional assistance. However, who ever heard of a Jewish geologist? Israel was about the last place in the world where you might find one.

Typical of the way things developed in those days, we had a choice of three geologists within a week. One was Professor Leo Picard of Hebrew University and two others were new immigrants who had heard that we might need some help. It didn't take long to learn that, as is so often the case, there were ways to solve our problem, but the solutions were expensive.

Then I recalled a rumor that the government wanted to close Haifa Airport and were looking for a buyer. The airport was an ideal site for the new plant. It was near the sea and hence cooling water would be readily available. It was also near the refineries that would be supplying gases for one of the processes. Most important of all, it was built on sand, which was an ideal material for foundations.

There were only two disadvantages. We would have to buy the airport and then move our new superphosphate plant to the new site.

A visit to the airport confirmed the fact that it was for sale and then I had a memorable visit with Sasha, which was typical of the way he did business. First, I explained all of the information and what was certainly a radical solution to the problem. Without any comment he picked up his phone and asked his secretary to get him the minister of transport—Mr. David Remez.

A minute or two later he had the minister on the phone and after the usual amenities he said: "David, I want to buy your airport in Haifa; how much do you want for it?" He got an answer on the spot, and noted it on a piece of paper. After his conversation with the minister he handed me the paper and said with a smile, "Now you figure out if it's worthwhile at this price." Sasha's willingness to consider the unconventional and the speed with which he dealt with the problem amazed me, but this was typical of the way Sasha worked.

It took two weeks to figure out that the airport option would be too costly, but getting negative results to proposed solutions was part of my job. Gradually we began to resolve our technical problems and we developed a master plan for the new chemical works. We then began to develop the budget required and the estimated return on the investment.

About this time, without our really noticing anything special, we slowly began to feel the effects of the enormous effort to absorb immigrants by a country with no real economic means. In my little office, which had no heat, I gradually became used to working in my overcoat and hat. Then, one day a visitor was shown into my room and his first comment was; "How can you work in a refrigerator?" It was only then that I realized that my working conditions were somewhat extraordinary.

It was at the beginning of April that the government announced that because of the lack of foreign currency no industrial raw materials had been imported the last four months of 1949. This, of course, meant that local industry was having an extremely difficult time. However, one didn't need the newspaper to know that Israel was beginning to be short of almost everything we normally take for granted.

For example, at Fertilizers and Chemicals we had a shortage of paper, and in my work I seemed to consume enormous amounts. As things began to become awkward, I began to look for some alternate arrangement and found that used envelopes were just the thing. From then on, the girl who opened the mail saved all the envelopes for me. I then unfolded these so that I could use what had been the inside for scrap paper.

Food was where the shortages hit home and about this time rationing became a way of life. Meat was one of the first items to become short. Each adult was allowed 125 grams—.275 pounds—of beef a week. Moreover, one did not have the choice that one would find in the average butcher shop abroad.

After receiving your ration cards, the butcher would turn to a large lump of red stuff and whack off a piece of the approximate size. Differences in weight were adjusted by adding or subtracting small bits. Obviously, the housewife would attempt to stretch the allotment as best she could. Steaks and the usual cuts of meat were unavailable except in one interesting case.

About that time, a friend of ours, Harry Beilin, became quite ill and needed a blood transfusion so Vic and I went to the local blood bank

(Mogen David Adom—Red Star of David). The facilities were very modest, but certainly adequate. A nurse with a star of David on her cap took our blood and then offered us the traditional glass of orange juice. After we had finished and started out the door the nurse called; "Wait a minute; don't you want your meat coupons?"

When we returned she explained that we each rated coupons for 1 kilo—2.2 pounds—of beef, too good to be true. After giving us the coupons she pointed to a butcher across the street and explained that that was the place to collect our ration.

When we walked into the shop the butcher greeted us with: "What will you have?" Just like in the States. Thinking this was a joke I said, "I'd like a steak." He didn't say a word, and took out of the fridge a big piece of red stuff that looked like a fillet of beef. He carefully weighed the meat and wrapped it in newspaper and handed me my "steak." It all seemed like a big joke.

By the time I got home, however, I began to wonder if this had really been a joke or did he really give us a fillet? This presented us with a problem, for we hadn't seen meat like this since living in Israel. If it was really a steak we didn't want to ruin it by cooking it as a pot roast. On the other hand if it were a pot roast, and we cooked it as steaks we wouldn't be able to chew them. What to do?

Live a little. We'd take a chance. I cut the meat into steaks as I remembered from the dim distant past, and Marilyn made us a steak dinner. The big moment came when we tasted the steaks and to our great pleasure these were the real thing. More surprising was the way Davy instinctively knew that these were something special. He had never tasted anything like fillet steak, but something told him that these were very good and he managed to eat two steaks.

Then the unprecedented occurred. On 29 January 1950 it snowed. Haifa never has snow, thus when about an inch of snow greeted us one morning, everyone was completely entranced. From Fertilizers and Chemicals it looked like Haifa was covered with a brilliant white sheet. This was such a great event that the schools closed to allow the kids to go out and actually touch this strange material.

By ten in the morning it was all gone but everyone was exhilarated to have actually seen snow in Haifa. Then, a week later on 6 February, we had a real blizzard (50 centimeters or 19 inches). Everything stopped. All traffic was trapped in drifts, and those of us who lived up on top of the Carmel had to trudge home through the snow.

For the next two days it was like a public holiday, for nothing could move. On the streets one got the impression that we were in Switzerland, not only because of the snow but because suddenly people began to appear on skis. Many Europeans who had skied in their youth had skis packed away in store rooms and suddenly they were taken back to the days of their youth. For about a day and a half we had skiing on Mount Carmel, but then the weather got back to normal and the snow hasn't been seen since.

At one time, Four Bashir had central heating, but it was not operable most of the time, which left all the residents on their own, insofar as heating was concerned. Our two-story living room was impossible to heat so we reluctantly closed it during the cold months and had a little kerosene heater in our entrance hall that became our living and dining room. Since this was a tiny area we stayed warm, but we never did find a solution to the odor of kerosene.

Life for the new immigrants living in tents had now become almost impossible. The government tried to alleviate some of their hardships, but the necessary resources were simply not available. Among other things, a campaign for established residents to take youngsters into their homes for the rest of the winter was initiated, and over seven thousand families answered the call. However, in view of the enormity of the problem, this was really a very small gesture.

Actually, the winter's difficulties were like the tip of an iceberg; one only saw a small part of the overall mass of problems. However, it is important to realize that despite our difficulties we all attempted to lead some sort of normal life.

Our social life was very extensive with a large circle of friends and frequent social evenings. The papers were filled with articles on the latest books, the latest films, the new circus in Tel Aviv, and sports. Even in those days Israel had its representatives in the Davis Cup tennis matches. Thus, although life was hard, we certainly did not sit around feeling sorry for ourselves. On the contrary, building a country and every tiny bit of progress gave us pleasure, compensating to a degree for some of the hardships.

Actually the whole process of austerity was just beginning and would become much much worse. On the other hand, Israel was slowly showing signs of beginning to cope with some of its problems.

# 25
# Negotiations Collapse

As winter turned to spring in 1950, we began to finalize our plans for F&C's new chemical complex; our work began to center on the financial problems. All of the various proposals from the foreign contractors and plans to develop the site had to be merged into an overall financial plan. This in turn had to be approved by the board of directors.

It seemed that each week I would complete the plan, which was around twenty pages of calculations, and go over it with Sasha. Then he would go off to a board meeting where the directors would discuss the plan.

Then the following day Sasha and I would sit together and he would say with a rueful smile, "Hal, I'm sorry, but you'll have to do it all over again." There was always someone who wanted to make some changes. The new calculations would usually take a week or so and, off Sasha would go to the next meeting.

Then, one day, things took a completely different turn. Sasha called me in and started out by saying, "Hal, I hate like the devil to tell you this, but I must be fair with you. Yaacov Lublini, the head of Vulcan Foundries, called to ask me if I would mind if they offered you a job." He went on to explain that Vulcan was expanding their steel fabrication plant and were even considering a shipyard. Apparently Lublini had made a point of the fact that I was better suited to running this new facility than working in a chemical plant.

Sasha continued by explaining that he did not want to lose me, but thought that, for my sake, I at least ought to go see them. This was really a bolt out of the blue and I was not paticularly interested in changing jobs, but I did make an appointment to visit Vulcan and found the experience quite intriguing.

Vulcan consisted of three main divisions: an iron foundry, a machine shop, and a steel fabrication plant. Each division was more or less independent, but shared the same top management and service facilities. The fabrication plant looked like the original maspenah with its broken-down sheds and antiquated machinery. However, every sizable project in the north was built by Vulcan, as were major projects over the rest of the country.

They were very proud to show me the start of a new fabrication plant, which was huge. Much of the new machinery was already on the way, and, as they put it, I would have lots of lovely new toys to keep me busy. The whole experience was very flattering and I was quite tempted. However, it did not seem right to leave Sasha at such a critical time, so I politely declined and went back to tell Sasha my decision. His reaction was, "Thank God."

So back I went to figuring out all the ways one could go about building a fertilizer plant, and it seemed that the indecision and wrangling of the board would never end.

The first of May was a memorable comedy of errors. Israel being a labor-oriented country, took the first of May—Labor Day—very seriously, complete with red flags and a big parade. Also on that same day one of the first tourist ships of the season arrived in Haifa Port to be greeted with hundreds of big red flags flying in the breeze.

The average Israeli considered the flags quite appropriate since the red flag had been labor's symbol since the French Revolution. However, to the Americans on the ship, red flags could only mean one thing: communism. No amount of explanation would convince them that Israel was hardly a Communist country and many of our potential visitors were damned if they would go ashore in a "Communist" country.

During this period there seemed to be a major shift in our daily news. Most of the front pages of our papers began to feature foreign news such as the war in Korea. The Israeli news also changed in character. Military incidents became much less frequent and more of a terrorist nature. We would read about trucks going over mines that had been planted by infiltrators and isolated shootings.

On the twelfth of May, 1950, a little remembered event occurred that set the pattern for many many similar occurrences over the next twenty years. We read in our papers:

Youth Shot Dead by Arab Legionnaire

It seems that a young boy was collecting scrap, near the border between Israeli and Jordanian Jerusalem, and wandered into no man's land. Whereupon, the Transjordan soldier simply shot him. It should be realized that the Transjordan Legion was still led by British officers and it was hard for Israelis to accept that when a youngster strayed into the sights of a Jordanian soldier, he became fair game for murder.

Unfortunately, for years to come we were to hear over and over again that when some innocent person strayed across the dividing line, the legionnaires simply killed him.

Immigration was still a major issue, for everyone was convinced that with the new Jewish State we had to bring the majority of the world's Jews to Israel. Thus we really took great pride in such 1949 headlines as:

| | |
|---|---|
| 19 March | Yemen Migration Almost Completed |
| 10 May | India's Immigrants Arrive by Plane |
| 21 May | Jews from China Arrive at Lydda |
| 23 May | First Baghdad Planes Arrive |
| 9 June | Israelis Bear Financial Brunt of Absorbing Immigrants |
| 20 June | U.S. Orders 108 Refugees Deported |
| 21 August | Immigration from Eight Countries Completed [Germany, Austria, Bulgaria, Yugoslavia, Czechoslovakia, Poland, Yemen, Cyrenaica (eastern Libya)] |
| 27 August | Plane Load of Immigrants from Hadhramaut [Adren] Arrives |

As one can see these were not just the remnants of European Jewry. These immigrants also came from the near and far east, places that we had never associated with oppressed Jewish populations.

The Baghdad story was of particular interest because it was here that we saw the real plight of Jews living in some Arab countries. The Jewish community of Iraq was one of the most well-to-do in the world, yet they had to leave everything behind. The chance to leave was not to be missed, so leave they did.

The story about the U.S. government deporting 108 Jewish refugees from Europe was a real puzzler, particularly in light of what we saw everyday. Apparently, these particular refugees did not have visas, and, when they arrived in New York, the immigration authorities insisted that there was no way that they could be allowed into the United States. Thus, on this technicality they were returned to Europe where they had to start over again looking for a new home.

As one might expect, the enormous influx of people, and the virtually nonexistent industrial base meant that more and more shortages were bound to occur in these months of 1950.

6 April      Meat and Sugar Cut but Fish, Eggs, and Vegetables Increased

23 June      No Meat this Week

6 July      More Furniture on Market Soon

13 July      One Chocolate Bar, Half Bar of Soap

16 July      More Austerity Ahead—[Ben Gurion]

31 July      Clothing and Shoes to Be Rationed

One of the more subtle effects of the influx of refugees was the shortage of furniture. Since the overwhelming majority of new immigrants arrived with little more than the clothes on their backs, they soon needed furniture. However, it was not long before there was nothing left in the shops to buy. Since the government did not have the foreign currency to import raw materials, the various workshops could not supply the demand, even for the most basic items.

The headline of 6 July refers to a government plan to cope with this problem. Special low-cost furniture requiring a minimum of materials was planned and for such items the government was prepared to allow the import of the necessary materials. Gradually, this approach to austerity products was used to include clothing and all sorts of other items.

Half a bar of soap per person per month was the sort of thing that let you know that things were going to get worse before they got better. We weren't to be disappointed.

From this sort of background one can see that the economy and its development were basic to the survival of the country and many of us followed such news with almost fanatic interest. Unfortunately, it was premature to expect whole industries to appear, but there was progress, and some of the developments of 1950 were quite interesting.

4 April      100-Day Shoe Plant Will Be Jerusalem's Largest Factory

24 July      Kaiser Fraizer Plant Parts Arriving

18 May      Money in Waste Materials

10 August      Middle East's First Grain Elevator to be Built at Haifa Port

23 August      100 Firms Passed by Investment Center

25 August     Old American Refrigerators Rebuilt in New Haifa
              Plant


The Jerusalem Shoe Company performed their own miracle by
building their plant, training the workers, and starting production, all
within one hundred days. Kaiser Fraizer was an American auto assembly plant that also went into production in record time. These factories, together with the grain elevator, were strictly in the big leagues,
but the little plants showed some interesting creativity.

In May, Mr. Leo Hirchenhauser, who had made his fortune in the
scrap business in the United States, came on a visit and found that no
one was exploiting the vast amounts of scrap to be found in Israel. He
maintained that a good living could be made collecting scrap and he
would help set up over one hundred people as scrap merchants. Each
received a horse and wagon, plus a baling press. Even today we see
scrap collectors making their rounds. Most of the horses and wagons
have been replaced by small tenders, but Mr. Hirchenhauser made his
mark.

Another innovative enterprise was David Kestenbaum's refrigerator
plant. In essence, old junked refrigerators were imported to Israel
where they were rebuilt and sold to refrigerator-starved Israelis. The
plant was well equipped and produced a very acceptable product—five
refrigerators a day. There were very few refrigerators in the country at
that time, so Mr. Kestenbaum's little factory filled a very important
need.

Another small addition to Israel, but a most important one to the
Gershoni household, was the appearance of Jonathan Gershoni on the
thirtieth of August. The whole approach to childbirth was very different than in the United States; however, Marilyn readily adjusted to
the local conditions. Considering the fact that David had been born at
one of New York's most modern hospitals, this showed a lot of the
spirit of the day.

On the one hand, there were thousands of babies being born to
refugees to whom the Israeli facilities were far superior to anything
they had seen in recent years, but to the young women who had come
from New York, London, or Cape Town, the situation was somewhat
different. Israeli hospitals were very limited insofar as equipment was
concerned, and necessities such as incubators were not always available. However, most of our friends were having children. Looking
back, these young women really deserved a lot of credit. They too
were pioneers.

Then toward the end of August, Sasha returned from a board

meeting and announced that they could not get together with the government on the conditions for the new plant. Since they saw no solution to the impasse, it was decided not to go ahead with the plant. Moreover, Sasha was not well and required an operation in England. My job had suddenly evaporated.

However, Sasha had discussed the situation with Vulcan, and the job as head of their fabrication department was still open if I wanted it. Thus within a few days I was working at Vulcan Foundries.

An interesting footnote to the F&C story is that Sasha did go off to England for his operation. A week before he was to have gone into the hospital, however, he read in the paper that the U.S. government was about to grant a large sum of money to Israel for the development of agriculture. On seeing this source of capital, he notified his doctor that he didn't have time for the operation and flew to Washington instead.

There he managed to convince the authorities that one couldn't have agriculture without fertilizer and that it was only logical to invest some of the grant to build the new plant. As usual, Sasha was most convincing and did manage to get sufficient backing to go ahead with the F&C nitrates project. Today F&C is one of Israel's largest companies.

# 26
# Dreams Start Coming True

Looking back at the year September 1950–September 1951, it is plain that four interdependent factors were at work.

Immigration
Threat of War
Austerity
Building the Economy

Originally, we had looked at the immigration problem as one primarily concerned with bringing the remnants of European Jewry to their home, Israel. However, we now began to see that this was only a part of a much broader problem.

(1950)

| | |
|---|---|
| 4 September | 1,400,000 Want to Come; Urgent to Save 600,000 from Destruction—Ben Gurion |
| 7 September | 12% of Population to Spend Winter Under Canvas |
| 6 December | Soldiers Rushed to Camps to Bolster Swamped Camps |

(1951)

| | |
|---|---|
| 8 January | Youth Aliyah Children Come from 67 Nations |
| 29 January | 90,000 More Expected by Iraq Air Lift |
| 13 March | Iraq Air Lift Arrivals Report Fear of New Anti-Jewish Laws |
| 26 June | 70,000 in Iran Next on List to Emigrate to Israel |
| 11 July | Iran to Make Jews Leave |
| 27 July | Share with All Who Come—Golda |

10 September     Israelis Will Allow No Immigration Curb

19 September     500,000 African Jews in Danger


To us, these were not just headlines, for we lived amid the ideals of rebuilding the Jewish Homeland and the ingathering of the exiles. People were pouring into the country and Israel was completely unequipped to deal with such a flood.

There was a desperate shortage of housing, and most newcomers were living in huge tent cities. That winter was unusually cold and wet and life in these camps was extraordinarily difficult. Life's necessities were scarce, but we could not stop immigration. The wealthy countries displayed a luxury we could ill afford; they simply refused to accept refugees.

The headlines of 27 July and 10 September really summarize the whole situation. We would bring all who wanted to come and would share what we had. I really cannot recall any dissent against this policy.

The military problem was also entering a new phase. Ostensibly we had cease-fires with our neighbors, and there were endless talks and negotiations for a proper peace. However, the hostilities did not end and we were constantly under attack.


(1950)

1 September     Army Patrol Routs Mine Layers

2 October     Dum Dum Bullets Killed Boy—Jerusalem

29 November     Israeli Youth Killed and Two Injured While Standing on Veranda of Home—Jerusalem

3 December     Israel Convoy Removes Elath Roadblock, Legion Withdraws

17 December     Arab Legion Sentry Kills Youth; Marauders Murder Immigrant


(1951)

11 January     'All Ahram' Claims 'State of War'

4 February     Arabs Shoot Another Jerusalem Resident, Second in Two Days

11 February     Ex-Mufti Urges War on Israel

5 April        7 Israeli Police Killed, 3 Hurt by Syrian Troops
               Inside Israel

20 June        Arab Press Renews Call for War Against Israel

The headlines more or less speak for themselves, but there is a most important point to be noted. Here we see the start of an endless parade of hostility in which the Arab leaders continuously proclaimed that they would not tolerate Israel in their midst. No week passed without them declaring that they would push us into the sea. The various attacks and violence punctuated their threats. Under such conditions we had little choice but to devote enormous energy and resources to national defense.

Faced with these two demanding problems, immigration and defense, Israel's tiny economy was strained far beyond capacity and this meant the intensification of the austerity. In this regard every Israeli felt the effects as everyday facts of life.

(1950)

4 October      All-Out War on Black Market

2 November     Cure for B.M.

1 December     Streptomycin and Penicillin Scarce

19 December    Shortages Hurt Steel Factories


(1951)

12 January     Paper Bus Money to Disappear Soon

6 March        Israel at Bottom of U.S. List for Vital Sulfur, Shut
               down New Fert. Plant in Haifa

7 June         Water Rations Twice Weekly in Jerusalem

12 July        Tel-Aviv Sets up Ice Rationing

20 July        Water Shortage Hits Tel-Aviv

3 August       Milk Must Be Boiled, Doctors Warn; No Fresh
               Milk for Adults

10 August      Fruits, Vegetables Short in Jerusalem


What in the world could the headline "Cure for B.M." mean? I asked myself the same question when going back over the papers of those days. Then I read the letter of a very irate citizen who complained that his newborn son was stricken with very serious bowel problems and his doctor had prescribed mixing cornflower with the child's milk. However, there was no cornflower to be found.

Fortunately, there were relatives in the states; and a cable was sent to rush cornflower by air. The only trouble with this solution was that the package arrived in Israel in one day, but was not cleared by the customs for a month. At this point I jumped to the end of the letter and was completely amazed to find that I had written this letter.

Actually, I remembered this incident, but for another reason, which did not appear in the newspaper. The cable was greeted in the United States with all sorts of questions as to what was wrong with the new baby and my parents immediately sought out the family doctor. Apparently, cornflower was not considered food for newborns in Great Neck, even when they had diarrhea, but then the good doctor came up with the probable answer. Jonny must have a rash and the cornflower was to be applied externally.

He went on to add that there were much better skin preparations than cornflower, and he gave the folks a dozen samples of such products. Fortunately, however, my father announced, "If Harold asked for cornflower, he meant cornflower and we're also going to include cornflower in the package."

What do you do when the doctor says your child is seriously ill and that he must have four doses of penicillin, but then adds that there is virtually none available? You do what we did; you go from pharmacy to pharmacy praying that you will find the child the medicine he needs. Yes, we were lucky but many others did without.

Paper bus money was exactly what the name implies. Coins virtually disappeared from the market. People could not pay the bus drivers, and they, in turn, could not make change. What to do? The bus cooperatives printed their own paper coins, and for months these grubby bits of paper became a substitute for money.

Every phase of our daily lives was plagued with shortages and one can see that many of the headlines not only refer to basic personal necessities, but to industrial raw materials as well.

The obvious answer to most of these problems was a large injection of money into the economy. Fortunately, in the fall of 1950 things began to move in this direction. At the end of October a billion-dollar program was initiated, which resulted in the Israel Bonds drive; and at about the same time the United Jewish Appeal began to raise large sums for Israel.

These two programs were significant for two reasons. First, this huge injection of capital gave Israel the possibility to buy raw materials and to finance many of the projects necessary to build an economy. Second, these funds were based on gifts and loans from American Jews as distinguished from U.S. government aid.

It is important to realize that, until this time, most of the burden of building the country and settling refugees had been carried by the Israel population. Loans and grants from the U.S. government were still in the future. Then suddenly we had partners, the Jews in America, and the entire picture changed.

With the influx of funding, many of the plans on paper came to life. All sorts of new plants began to appear making everything from asphalt to zippers. The public was certainly aware of new products like refrigerators, cars, pencils, and more electricity for such items were seen in our daily life.

On the other hand, the average citizen was unaware of all sorts of new and vital industrial products such as Ytong, welding electrodes, cement, electric motors, and bricks, which were beginning to be made locally. A vast array of new enterprises began to appear and Vulcan was very busy building these factories.

The range of Vulcan's projects was almost without limit. We added all sorts of new buildings and equipment to the Vulcan complex including our own new steel fabrication shop. Steel City near Acre also came into being, which included a steel mill plus several pipe mills; Vulcan built the buildings and conveyors for these plants.

Any firm requiring a boiler obtained it from Vulcan. Tanks and vessels for the chemical industry were also made in great quantities. Elaborate conveyor systems for the Kaiser Fraiser automobile plant and the Nesher cement plant were built. The new power plant in Tel Aviv and additions to the power plant in Haifa were also made by Vulcan. When the port required new barges, these too were manufactured by Vulcan.

All of these products were manufactured by Vulcan's steel fabrication department, but it should be remembered that Vulcan also had the largest iron foundry in the Middle East, plus a very respectable machine shop. These other departments were also loaded to capacity. One interesting product combining all of these departments was concrete mixers and this line was greatly expanded.

We truly did deliver the goods but, because the economy was in its infancy, there were endless problems. The first pipe mill in Acre seemed to run the gamut of everything that could go wrong. Since the overall program for the new plant was far behind schedule, one of the conditions for our receiving the contract for the buildings was that we had to work according to a very rigid schedule. This was the time to show the American approach to production.

All during the fabrication of the various trusses and building parts I harped away at the need to be on time, but the project seemed to have a will of its own. All sorts of basic tools were not available and this led to endless makeshift arrangements. However, with some items, such as fifty-meter measuring tapes, expedients are not acceptable: you needed the real thing. Thus, when we found that there was only one tape left, we hit one of the first major crises. All we needed was for someone to step on this last tape and we would be unable to continue. We finally did get tapes from abroad, but walked on eggs until these arrived.

Such were the little problems. Then one day it appeared that our crane was not suited to travel on sand, but the building was to be built on such a site. Locating another crane of this size was not very likely, but, on looking through the catalog for one crane, I came across the solution to our problem. Apparently, such cranes were sent to Saudi Arabia, which had similar problems. The solution suggested was to deflate the tires to a very low pressure that would enable the crane to roll over sand.

Instinct said, "Try this now while there's time." So one morning we drove the crane to a sandy lot next to Vulcan, deflated the tires, and then drove onto the sand only to find that this twenty-ton crane became hopelessly stuck. Fortunately, some bulldozers were working across the road and were able to pull the crane back to the road.

The most practical solution was to visit a friend in the army corps of engineers who immediately offered to lend us some steel matting that could be laid on the sand as a temporary roadway.

Then a week before we were supposed to start erecting the building, we found that there was no truck available to cart the trusses from the plant to the site. This was no simple matter, for in those days there were only three trucks in the country large enough to move such long loads. Solving this was routine. First, I screamed, then various others screamed, until Solel Boneh agreed to let us have the truck when needed.

These were routine problems, but then a much more basic problem arose. The erection foreman in charge of the building came to me with a very long face about a week before the big day and said, "We can't make it, there are no half-inch bolts."

To an American this was utterly idiotic, for I still did not fully understand how bad things really were. Then started a long list of suggested solutions.

Try the shops in Haifa, or Tel Aviv. They had already done this.

How about the factory that manufactures bolts?" They won't be making half-inch bolts for another three weeks.

Make them in the machine shop. We thought of that, but there is no material and there's none available on the market.

I suggested a long list of possibilities only to be given very sound reasons why each idea would not work. I must have ended up by saying, "For heaven's sake, use some ingenuity," for about two hours later the foreman was back.

He greeted me with a wan smile and the comment, "It's OK. I have the bolts." From his look I got the impression that something wasn't quite right and asked: "Where did you get them?" Whereupon he replied, "Better you don't know." At which point I of course insisted on knowing. He really had used ingenuity.

As he explained, "You know the main foundry building has a roof the same as the one we're building in Acre. The trusses are held together with gusset plates each having twelve bolts, so I borrowed one from each gusset plate in the foundry." At first I had visions of the entire foundry collapsing, but, after calming down a bit, I realized that the safety factor was more than sufficient. So, after extracting a promise to replace the bolts as soon as these became available, I gave the OK to go ahead.

It has often occurred to me that someday someone will notice a very strange thing about Vulcan Foundry's roof in that every gusset is probably still missing a half-inch bolt.

Of course we weren't the only ones with problems; every phase of everyone's life was rife with such problems. On the other hand one should not misconstrue the way we lived. Despite such problems we enjoyed life. In addition to all sorts of social activities the community itself had its lighter side.

(1950)

27 September    Third World Maccabia Opens Today
                Top Jewish Sports Teams of World

(1951)

8 January       Gala Concert, Yehudi Menuhin

22 April        Peace and Music at Ein Gev Passover Music Festival

30 May          Chagall Exhibit Opening Today in Jerusalem, Largest Ever Held

31 May          40,000 See Soccer Match, Dundee Beats Maccabi 2:0

| 18 July | Dodgers Increased Their Lead Over Giants in National League to 9 1/2 Games |
| 29 July | Haifa Goes to the Sea Shore, Preelection Weekend |
| 22 August | Pageant of Splendor Enthralls Thousands at Kibbutz Dalia |

People did what people do everywhere, and our papers featured all sorts of entertainment as well as the grim news of the day. We read of concerts and all sorts of public entertainment, and the sports pages were filled with news from all over the world. In essence we did our best to live normal lives.

The secret of remaining sane was to believe in what we as a nation were building. Thus, despite the frustrations of daily life, there were also compensations. We took great pride in the happenings of the day and perhaps got a bit of extra pleasure because these were a part of the new nation we were building.

# 27
# Vulcan Foundries

In order to relate to Vulcan as a real place, a word or two on its history is most important. Vulcan had been originally established by a German Zionist named Kreminer who believed that the Jewish State would need a large iron foundry. He employed over five hundred workers and produced all sorts of basic products ranging from bathtubs to machine parts. The only problem was that the tiny economy preceding the Jewish State could not really support such a plant and the owner was faced with bankruptcy.

At this point, the Histadrut—the labor union—stepped in. Today one hears the slogan, We're in Business to Make Money, but, thank heavens, the Histadrut was in business to look after the interests of their workers and to build the Jewish State. They took over the plant and ran it at a loss for many years to make sure that their members had work, and equally important, to insure that the country had a proper iron foundry.

This policy of the Histadrut was most important, for it not only kept a significant number of workers employed, but it preserved their specialized skills. Later, when vital military equipment was all but unobtainable abroad, Vulcan became an important supplier for the armed forces. Actually, this was the background to many enterprises that were supported at that time by the workers themselves. Today there is talk about unfair competition to private industry, but in those days only the Histadrut stepped forward to take the risk of preserving such vital facilities.

The pay was low as behooved a workers' establishment, but there were advantages as well. Every worker had a secure job; layoffs simply did not occur. Moreover, the management was actively concerned about the employees' welfare. For example, on my first day at work someone came into the office and placed a bottle of milk on my desk. When I asked what this was all about, I was given a long explanation about how the fumes of the foundry and welding shop were harmful to health and how the milk counteracted the ill effects.

Years later I learned that this was a ploy to insure that a bit of necessary nourishment reached every employee each day. Similarly, the canteen was subsidized to make sure that their employees, who supported so many families, would have at least one proper meal each day.

Despite the explanations about health hazards, it was noted that, as the food situation became more critical, workers often put the milk bottles in their lunch boxes for the kids at home. Thus we soon had our milk in glasses poured from a pitcher to force everyone to drink it on the spot.

This preoccupation for keeping the workers fit was, of course, a direct result of the worsening food situation. It was about this time that CARE packages were beginning to arrive; these furnished a welcome addition to the rations of many families. The Gershonis also received one or two packages and the contents were an important contribution to our diet. Each ten-dollar package contained:

2 pounds Beef
15 ounces Veal
1 pound Butter
1 pound Cheese
2 pounds Salmon
2 pounds Milk Powder
29 ounces Rice
1 pound Coffee
3 pounds Vegetable Shortening

One of the most interesting food packages, however, was something quite different. One day we received a package from Marilyn's uncle Leo, which had a very special character. In this package we found a selection of twelve gourmet soups. Each was quite delicious and his thought of something elegant to perk up our meals was greatly appreciated.

Vulcan, in those days, was terribly outdated, particularly when compared to similar plants in the United States. This too deserves a word or two of explanation. Israeli industry had been working in a vacuum for many years and most of the great strides made in the United States during the war were completely unknown to local manufacturers. Moreover, many of the primitive methods were used because no other choice existed.

For example, one day I met a new friend, Isaac Minkoff ("Minky"). He was about my age, and from England, and served in both the British Army and then the Israeli Army, and most important, he was a first-class metallurgist. Minky worked in the laboratory of the foundry and on that first meeting he was virtually ready to explode.

In any normal foundry the chemical analysis of the iron castings is adjusted to the optimum composition by mixing various batches of raw materials. At Vulcan, however, no attempt was made to check the analysis of the raw materials, which to Minky, was absolutely insane. How could they neglect such a basic approach to sound foundry practice?

The true picture was a bit different, however, and it took us both some time to realize what was really happening. Actually, there was no foreign currency available to buy a proper selection of raw materials. If we were lucky enough to import a small quantity of iron, that was all we had, so that was what they melted. There was no point in checking the analysis when there was only one batch of metal available.

My experience with both the management and the workers at Vulcan was quite positive. We did not always agree on my sometimes radical approaches to the work, but everyone was very much interested in improving the plant and its methods. This was a real challenge for a young engineer, and to my great pleasure, the management was very willing to cooperate. Thus, during the next few months, in addition to filling all sorts orders for our customers, we evolved into a modern steel fabrication plant.

During my very first days at Vulcan I asked to see the layout of the new factory that was already under construction. Sure enough, someone had laid out all the machinery on the drawing of the proposed building, but, unfortunately, had not thought to include the materials in the drawing. Because the materials often require far more space than the machines, the proposed layout was completely impossible. Something had to be done immediately.

Fortunately, the top management of Vulcan readily understood the problem, when it was explained, and were prepared to go along with the solution that required adding about 30 percent more space to the building and leaving out one department.

Another shock was Vulcan's use of forklifts. Someone had evidently seen pictures of these machines whisking materials from here to there in American factories and decided that these were just what were needed. Two machines were purchased, but the two machines were only a part of the equipment needed.

Normally, materials rest on pallets or skids (low platforms) and the forklift drives up to the load inserting the forks under the load. The forks are then raised lifting the load off the ground, and then the truck moves the work to the new location that can be onto a storage rack or on the floor beside a machine. In this latter case the worker would remove a piece from the skid, process it, and then place it on an empty skid. When the lot is finished, the forklift would move the loaded skid to the next location.

Since, no one had seen such equipment in action, the need for the skids was completely overlooked. At Vulcan the work was hand loaded piece by piece onto and off of the forks themselves. Thus what normally is a very efficient method of shifting materials, became a labor intensive time-consuming nightmare.

The first step was to design a simple skid and order a dozen for testing. However, when I gave my sketch and order to David Greenspoon, the foreman, he looked at the order and said: "Why twelve when we only have two trucks?" Since I was preoccupied with other problems, I simply mentioned that it would soon be obvious and he left rather puzzled.

The first skids seemed OK so I gave him another order for twelve skids and this really puzzled Greenspoon. "You already have twelve skids for only two trucks and now you want to make another twelve?"

However, after another week, when the second lot were already being digested, Greenspoon asked me to sign a work order for another twenty-four skids. This time I feigned shock and said, "You've only got two trucks and already have twenty-four skids; what's going on?" In turn he laughed and said, "You know very well why I need them." It was not long until we had hundreds of skids and the place began to look like an American factory.

This really exemplified what was happening in Vulcan and in the entire country. Many of our firms had not been exposed to modern methods and thus had no way of knowing any better. However, when people saw what could be done they readily grasped modern technology.

In many cases it was only necessary to aim people in the right direction. For example, our welding foreman, Cohen, was a first-class craftsman and also a very clever fellow. However, the concept of holding the parts to be welded in jigs, to make things easier for the welder, was completely foreign to him. In this case the transition was like an explosion. We talked about the problem and the possibility of using old ball bearings in various types of jigs so that the welders could rotate the work. From that moment Cohen took over.

Everywhere one turned, there were welding jigs. Then one day I noted that Cohen was on the verge of loosing his pants and he seemed to be much fatter than usual. When I questioned this, he laughed and began to take all sorts of old ball bearings out of his pockets. He was so taken with the idea of welding jigs, that he carried parts with him. Then, whenever he wanted to help one of his men with a new jig, he had what he needed in his pockets.

Insofar as the management was concerned, I soon learned that any new idea would be greeted with objections, but this was mainly because they needed time to digest new concepts. Thus I developed a special technique for them. Whenever I felt the need to initiate a change, such as a stock control or production control system, I would first write a one-page memo describing the innovation and its need.

The memo would be given to the management with no comment, but I soon learned that each one was well studied. Then a week or two later I would raise the subject at one of our meetings. By this time the idea was no longer strange and everyone had had time to think about it, so the reactions were mainly questions. Then in the following weeks we would work out the details.

Later I was sure that my memos were appreciated for a rather funny reason. One day we had a meeting of all the workers during which the management explained its plans for the future. At one point the general manager, Yaacov Lublini, began to explain all sorts of new ideas and suddenly I found that even with my very limited Hebrew I understood every word.

Then it dawned on me that the reason I understood was because he had translated my memos into Hebrew and in essence, I had written the speech.

By summer, things at Vulcan began to settle down. The new factory was in operation and the new organization began to function as a modern steel fabrication plant. During this period, perhaps because there was less pressure than before, I became fascinated with the possibilities of the lost wax casting process. This is a very ancient foundry technique that seemed to be ideal for Israel. In a sense, it could bypass many of the processes the country lacked and would enable us to produce all sorts of necessary products.

The lost wax process was actually used by the ancient Egyptians for casting gold scarabs. Before World War II it was used mainly by dentists for casting gold inlays and by goldsmiths for making jewelry. During the war, however, great progress was made in adapting this process to industrial castings of everything from aluminum to steel.

As I collected catalogs and data, a new dream was taking shape, although my interest was strictly academic, and I never had any intention of personally getting involved in a new enterprise. However, toward the end of the summer several things seem to come together that suddenly changed the situation and put me in the foundry business.

One evening, while visiting Lee and Leah Harris, I mentioned the subject, and to my amazement Lee was most interested. Lee was head of the Bayside Land Company that was developing industrial sites all over the country, and such a plant seemed just right for their new factory complex in the Haifa Bay area.

This social evening led to several other more serious meetings. Then one day Lee suggested that, if I wanted to go ahead with such a project, he would see that the funds were available and his company would supply the building. At first this was just interesting talk, for I was quite happy at Vulcan, but then we received a letter from the United States that changed the whole picture.

Our families had gotten together and invited us for a visit to the States and even included the tickets. However, to my chagrin, Vulcan was not prepared to release me for a month. It was then that the new foundry became most attractive. Thus, a few weeks later we found that the Gershonis were on their way to visit the States, and at the same time I would buy the equipment for a new precision foundry.

# 28
# Learning about Americans

Our first days back in the States were a wonderful reunion with family and friends. Davy and Jonny learned the joy of having grandparents, and it seemed that every evening we were wined and dined. It was then that we noticed one of the tolls of austerity; our stomachs had shrunk. After the first course and a bit of salad we would find that we were quite satiated and couldn't eat another bite. At which point our hostess would anxiously ask: "Is something wrong; would you prefer something else?" It was hard for them to understand that such a small part of their usual meal was far more than we normally ate.

Somewhere along the way we also learned that little Davy had become a terrible chauvinist. In Israel the cultivation of apples had just begun and the first products were pretty grim. Tiny little red things with multiple worm holes, and each apple had to be carefully pared before eating. Now suddenly, doting grandparents with much ado were offering huge "American" apples. Whereupon Davy would reply, "We have apples in Israel too!" Fortunately, Marilyn and I were the only ones who saw the humor in this.

My first task insofar as the new foundry was concerned, was to recruit the necessary capital; this turned out to be quite a simple job. Before leaving Israel, Lee Harris, and two of his associates, Matitiahu Borochov and Murray Greenfield, had each agreed to invest some money, and Lee had given me a list of friends to whom he had already written concerning the new enterprise.

My first meeting was with my college roommate, Ray Frankel, who was now an expert in hi-tech investments. After going over the figures, Ray became not only a partner, but our U.S. contact. Within a day or two, Lee's buddies also joined us and we were ready to begin the next phase that was quite an education—social as well as technical.

Our technical problems were mainly to locate specific equipment that would not only do the job, but would also fit Israel's special conditions. At the same time it was necessary to accumulate all sorts of technical know-how on the process. However, the social aspects were perhaps more interesting for I began to gain a much deeper appreciation of the American people.

Until this time I had considered the U.S. government and the American people to be one and the same. Hence, resentment of U.S. government policy carried over to a rather uncomfortable feeling about the American people. It should be remembered that in those days, U.S. policy toward Israel was quite different than it is today.

It seemed that the U.S. policy was based on currying favor with our Arab neighbors, and keeping us at arm's length. When the Arab leaders openly declared their intentions of pushing us into the sea, this was somehow overlooked. We were unable to obtain desperately needed military equipment, while England openly supplied our enemies. When we were attacked, the most we could expect in aid was an ineffectual protest at the United Nations. Our only ally at that time was the world's Jewish community.

From the standpoint of the naive, such as myself, this seemed most unjust. Israel had accepted the U.N. partition plan and had desperately tried to live up to its terms. On the other hand, our enemies flagrantly flaunted the United Nations. Israel was the only democratic country in the Middle East; and was certainly the only country on which the United States could count in a confrontation with the Communist block. It seemed insane, that under these circumstances, the United States would embrace our enemies.

Then, one day I happened to meet an American attorney who was a legal advisor to the Israeli foreign office. When I asked where the justice was in the U.S. policy, he explained that the situation had nothing whatsoever to do with justice. As he put it, U.S. officials were paid to look after the interests of the United States, and not those of Israel. Unfortunately, at that time, our neighbors had much more to offer the United States than we; hence, U.S. policy was often antagonistic to our interests.

Some years later I found a quotation, that puts this basic principle more eloquently. "It is a maxim, founded on the universal experience of mankind, that no nation is to be trusted further than it is bound by its interest; and no prudent statesman or politician will venture to depart from it" (George Washington).

With this in mind, and the knowledge of what had been happening during Israel's infancy, it is no great wonder that Israel's policy was greatly influenced for years to come. We felt then as today, "When the chips are down, we may well be on our own, so be ready." This was the logic behind establishing a national airline, large merchant marine, powerful army, and extensive agricultural development. In later years we would also build an armaments industry, manufacture tanks, and attempt to build fighter aircraft.

Looking back, this policy of preparedness saved our necks on more than one occasion. However, as I was to find during our U.S. visit, there were enormous differences between U.S. government policy and the views of the American people.

My first stop in assembling our equipment was Saginaw, Michigan, where I visited a manufacturer of electric arc furnaces. It seemed that we developed a special rapport from the very start. My hosts were most helpful and I soon decided that we should buy two furnaces, one small laboratory model, and also one with a one-hundred-pound capacity. This latter model was really tiny for industrial use, but some firms were using whole batteries of these furnaces.

The first crisis arose when I wanted to place an order, for I was informed that the delivery time was two years. This was a crushing blow, for we had to be in production within a period of months. In reply to this information I explained how we were frantically developing our industry and that this would be the first steel foundry in the entire country. We simply couldn't wait two years.

My host thought for a moment and then mentioned that he had an idea that might change things. Apparently General Motors had ordered one hundred of these furnaces to be delivered, one each week. The first shipment to General Motors was to be in a matter of days but he had a feeling that they might be prepared to let us have the first furnace. He then picked up the phone and called General Motors.

He explained our whole problem, stressing the fact that Israel was a new country and badly needed the furnace right away. The General Motors purchasing agent readily agreed that Israel needed this first furnace more than General Motors, and that they would be happy to help by letting us have the furnace.

It was not until the next evening, however, that I learned that this approach was more than a commercial gesture. The next evening before my plane back to New York was due, the chief engineer and his wife took me to dinner and then to the airport.

In those days the little planes taxied right up to the terminal and the passengers and friends could walk right up to the plane while saying their good-byes. My new friend shook hands and wished me well, and then, to my complete surprise, his wife kissed me on the cheek and said, "We really hope everything will be alright in Israel." She was trying to show me that they were truly concerned.

My next stop was at Union Carbide in New York where I hoped to buy carbon electrodes for the furnaces, and here our problems became even more difficult. I met with the sales manager and explained our new enterprise and that we would be needing several hundred carbon electrodes each year. He listened to my story and then replied that it would not be possible to supply us. These electrodes were used in the atomic energy program and simply were not available.

As in Saginaw, I explained the urgency of our problem, but this time it didn't help. As he was giving me his negative reply a new thought flashed through my mind. Perhaps we would make the electrodes in Israel. Then as a last resort I asked: "How do you make carbon electrodes?" Whereupon he burst out laughing, got up, walked over to a bookcase, selected a book, and handed it to me. He explained, "You can have this book. It tells everything about how to make electrodes, but, for heaven's sakes, don't try to make your own. It's much too complicated."

Then after a few seconds he said, "You know your demands are quite modest. I think that we ought to help you. Send me an order, and you can count on us to keep you supplied."

Well, things were certainly looking up, but there was more to come. One of our most important problems was with the supply of the ceramic investment used in making molds. In order to get started we would buy a whole carload of this material, but in the long run, we would have to learn how to make it ourselves.

The company producing the investment was very gracious about teaching me all about its use, but how to make it was another matter. Then a classmate from MIT, Sid Siegel, suggested that I contact a friend of his in the metallurgy department at MIT. Apparently they were involved in developing a new and better investment.

After calling to make an appointment, I went up to Cambridge and it really felt like coming home. Just walking down the corridors gave me a very pleasant feeling of nostalgia. My host in the metallurgy department was very cordial and quite interested in our plans for the plant in Israel. We talked about all sorts of problems that were bothering me and he was very forthcoming with information.

Then at one point he mentioned that he thought that our main problem would be to find some way of making our own investment, since it obviously would not be practical to import it from abroad. He then explained that they had been working on a new material that would be just right for Israel. He then excused himself for a few minutes, and on his return, invited me to his lab where I met his assistant.

He explained that she might be able to answer some of my questions concerning the investment. With that he excused himself again, explaining that he would join us later. The assistant was very pleasant and answered some of my questions, but then she went on to explain about their new investment. It apparently was a very simple compound. As a matter of fact, all the necessary details were written on one small file card, which she put down on the desk in front of me.

Then to my surprise, she explained that she had to see the boss and that she would be back in five minutes. Obviously, they could not tell me their secret of how to make the investment, but it was equally obvious that I was expected to copy the card, which I certainly did. Without question, it answered all my questions and the ingredients were all readily available at home.

At this point it must be explained that none of these kind people were Jewish and none had any special ax to grind. They were just good decent Americans who somehow identified with our problems and wanted to help. This was not on the level of the government policy; this was strictly a person to person activity.

I have often thought that Americans and Israelis are very similar. Both countries were founded by oppressed peoples, both are dedicated to building societies where such oppression would not flourish, and both peoples were pioneers. However, for whatever reason, I was most grateful and very proud of these Americans.

Interestingly enough, these sorts of incidents seemed to follow me about America. During our stay there was a foundry exhibition in Detroit, and this was just what I needed to complete my rather hurried education. The one thing that impressed me, however, was the way the various exhibitors received me. The minute they saw my name tag with the Israeli address, they were most enthusiastic. Everyone seemed to be following Israel's progress, and had all sorts of questions.

One question seemed to intrigue many people. "How long have you been here? Just six weeks? You certainly did learn English in a hurry."

Once the big problems such as furnaces and investment were settled, the rest was easy. We bought a lovely Plymouth station wagon, for now wheels were a necessity. The lesser items were all readily available and within a week or so our purchases for the factory were completed.

On the home front we were also busy buying, for in those days when one went abroad he carried a long shopping list of things that one could not obtain in Israel. Sears and Roebuck was one of our favorite sources and there we bought some rather special things.

Since pasteurized milk was not available in Israel, we bought a genuine home pasteurizer. Eggs were very much a luxury at the time but Marilyn, a city girl from Great Neck, New York, had heard that eggs come from chickens, and that one could raise chickens in the backyard. So back again to Sears where we bought an incubator and a small brooder to care for the newborn chicks.

The family thought most of these purchases somewhat strange, but later these things all came in very handy. Shipments to Israel were now quite routine and in a few days everything was in the hand of the freight forwarders and our vacation came to an end. Our good-byes this time were much less ominous than in 1948 and, since tourists were beginning to visit Israel, everyone promised to come and see us. Then before we knew what had happened, the Gershonis were on their way back to Israel.

# 29
# Dok Israel Precision Foundries

On our return to Israel, in the fall of 1951, we found little had changed. The country's problems were much the same, with immigration and the economy at the top of the list. The government remained adamant in its stand to accept all Jews who wanted to come. In retrospect, the one bright spot on the horizon was the fact that talks had started with the West German government on reparations.

We accepted the day-to-day problems, and rapidly settled back to our normal lives. The center of my thinking, however, was the progress of the new enterprise, and this was a wonderful education in what was really going on. In my previous positions I had always seen things from above as through a veil. Now I personally had to deal with all of the firm's day-to-day problems and it was like removing the veil. One got a very clear picture of how Israel's economy really functioned.

Since most people are not familiar with foundries, a very brief outline of the two processes used by "Dok" might be helpful. In sand casting, one packs a sand and clay mix around a pattern that is then removed, leaving a cavity exactly like the part required. Molten metal is then poured into the mold filling this cavity, and later the sand is removed leaving the rough casting. This is the most common process and makes rough castings that are then machined to size.

Investment casting starts with a wax model of the part required. If one is making many parts a simple metal mold is made of the part and numerous wax models can be made. The wax models are then covered with ceramic investment and when this has hardened, these molds are put in a furnace to melt the wax. With the wax removed, we now have a cavity exactly like the part to be cast. Molten metal is then poured into the hot mold. Later the ceramic is removed, leaving parts requiring very little finishing.

One of our first problems was to decide on a name for the company and this had interesting ramifications. The name had to be Hebrew, but pronounceable in English. However, there was a hidden problem. This came to light when we found just the right name but were

172

informed that Rumanians would be shocked by our vulgarity. Finally, we decided on Dok Israel Precision Foundries. The name *Dok* comes from the Hebrew word "precision" and seemed respectable in other languages, so Dok it was.

Lee Harris arranged for us to have a fine building in a new industrial park near Haifa where a number of other new plants were opening. One of my first new acquaintances was Nate Lepkin who had been in the piece goods business in Canada. He had decided that Israel needed a more down-to-earth industry, so he set up Tyresoles. This was as down-to-earth as one could get; his plant retreaded automobile and tractor tires.

One of the other plants was a fine little machine shop set up by two Italian immigrants. Here we had our first bit of culture shock. We needed some sort of part, and since our equipment had not yet arrived, I submitted a very carefully prepared drawing to this new machine shop. When the part was delivered, however, it did not even resemble the drawing.

It turned out that their numbers were different than mine, and they had mistaken every one of my sevens for a one. From then on, at the top of every drawing was "1, 2, 3, 4, 5, 6, 7, 8, 9, 0," to avoid any future mistakes. The Tower of Babel all over again. However, some of the problems were more amusing.

In our factory compound we had a very nice lunchroom where they did their best to provide meals with the limited foods available. One day the owner proudly informed me in his primitive Hebrew, "Today we've got pigless." He was constantly inventing all sorts of strange dishes, but this certainly did not sound appropriate. When I asked in my equally primitive Hebrew: "What's "pigless?" he explained that this was an English word and something very special. The whole thing didn't make any sense, so I ordered "pigless," and was handed a plate of pickles.

It took several months for machinery to start arriving and by this time the building and all the utilities were completed. At that time our entire staff consisted of Gershoni, who with the arrival of the first machines, became very busy opening the cases. Since wood, like everything else, was in very short supply, I took great care to remove the nails. Later we would be able to make use of the wood.

It was then that I was able to learn something of people who really came from technically backward societies. On that day I saw that what we in America thought was undeveloped was as far from the real case as night from day.

While working on my nail extractions, I noticed two young Arabs who indicated that they were looking for work. They spoke no Hebrew, and I no Arabic, but we did manage to communicate; I offered them the job of removing the nails. After carefully showing them exactly what I wanted, I handed each a simple clawhammer such as the ones used by carpenters. I expected that everyone would know what to do with a hammer. To be sure, some people have two left hands, but everyone knows more or less the general idea of what it is and how it's used.

Not in this case, however. At first, each took the hammer in their hands and it was obviously the first time they had ever seen one, much less used it. Over and over they turned it, examining it with great care. Then grabbing it at the head, and ignoring the handle completely, they tried to pull out nails. It soon dawned on me that the problem was not nearly as simple as I had imagined, and it wasn't long before I was again removing the nails.

A short time later Minky came to work and he was ideal for the job. He had a wonderful theoretical background and also lots of practical experience. One of Minky's first projects was to put us in the steel sand casting business. As he saw the situation, it would take us awhile to learn to produce precision castings; in the meantime, it would be worthwhile making some sand castings.

Normally one would call a foundry supply company and order the necessary sand, but we were in Israel and strictly on our own. Minky knew of a place up in the Western Galilee where the sand looked promising, so off we went. We found the place in the middle of nowhere, and filled the back of the station wagon with a good supply. After a few trials, we found the sand to be just fine and we were in business.

Simcha, our new toolmaker, was born in Germany and when Hitler came to power, he was all of twelve years old. He and his older brother soon found life intolerable. Since they had heard of organizations in England that would help youngsters who had managed to escape, they started out alone walking to the Channel. Somehow they got across to England and were taken in by such a Jewish organization. Then along came World War II and the two brothers wanted to do their part.

Simcha's brother went into the air force, but Simcha was much too young for the army. Then one day he saw an ad in the paper that was just the thing. Vickers had advertised for machine operators and this was the sort of job he was sure he could do. Here again we see a lovely case of person to person goodwill.

The personnel man at Vickers realized that this youngster was a special case and asked him what he would really like to do. Whereupon Simcha sighed and said, "I've always wanted to be a toolmaker." The interviewer replied, "Then that's what you're going to be." Simcha went through a five-year apprenticeship and became a first-class toolmaker.

Fortunately, it was not long before enough machinery arrived, to make it worthwhile to start employing a larger staff. Again, the "undeveloped countries" syndrome appeared. Virtually all of our new employees were from such places and training them for a hi-tech process revealed problems we never envisaged. The most impressive incident, perhaps, summarizes the whole situation.

As we began to operate our large furnace on a daily basis, we found that the time just to bring it up to temperature, consumed most of the working day. This left practically no time for the real business of making castings, so we decided to start up the furnaces at four in the morning. Our two furnace operators were quite pleased with this arrangement, for they lived nearby and would finish work early. Rehamim, a young immigrant from one of the Arab countries, was quite bright and was put in charge of this early shift.

Then one day, on our arrival, Minky, Simca, and I opened the door of the factory and immediately knew that the place was on fire. The odor was so strong that none of us even thought to discuss it; we simply ran to find the fire. The most logical place was the furnace, and sure enough, we found Rehamim standing there amid the smoke and the terrible odor completely unconcerned.

He had forgotten to turn on the cooling water that kept the electrodes from melting. As the electrode holders got hot, the insulation on the electric cables burned away and current began to arc across to the body of the furnace, thereby burning away more of the insulation.

It only took a minute or two to make the necessary repairs, but the real problem was why Rehamim let this potentially dangerous situation continue. When we asked why he didn't do anything, his reply was very simple. He didn't know that anything was wrong. Then when asked what he thought of the smoke, the odor, and the electric arc, he said that he didn't know that these were abnormal.

The next day was much the same with an interesting twist. This time, Rehamin had remembered to turn on the cooling water, but the damage from the previous day had been sufficient to cause the arcing and burning insulation to start up again, despite the cooling water. However, Rehamim had things in hand, so he thought. Water had solved every thing yesterday, so today he was standing there with a bucket of water, and was calmly splashing water over the electrical fire. We were completely shocked. Everyone knows that water and electrical fires don't go together. When we had put things back to rights again, we asked: "How could you do something not only stupid, but downright dangerous? You could have killed yourself."

This time, Rehamin was most upset with us and angrily replied: "How am I supposed to know about these things? Six months ago I lived in a tiny village that had no electricity. The first time I saw anything electrical was when I arrived in Israel." He was right; we had to start at the very beginning with all of our new workers.

Gradually, as the rest of the machinery arrived, we began to try out our new equipment. Now, anyone who has ever set up a new factory can tell you that the first six months will be a nightmare. All sorts of crises arise, and we fit right into this picture.

These starting up problems usually occur in great abundance and then disappear never to appear again. However, ours seemed to get mixed up with Israeli problems, which added to the confusion. First, one of our General Electric motors had a faulty starting switch, and a cable was sent to Ray Frankel. Within a day the switch was on its way by air, but it took this three-dollar switch a month to clear customs.

Some of the Israeli problems were infinitely more complex. Our large furnace was supposed to draw less than 200 amperes and we had had the electric company provide a 200-ampere service. We soon learned, however, that the furnace demand was not very stable and often went over 200 amperes. When this occurred, all the fuses in the neighborhood would blow. No one was very happy with this and the power company demanded that we either do something about the furnace or order a 500-ampere service.

A 500-ampere connection would have cost us a fortune, which we certainly did not have, so we began to ask who was the local expert on such matters. The universal answer was, "Lurie." So off I went, and meeting Mr. Lurie was indeed a shock.

His little workshop was not far from our plant, and there I found him to be a reincarnation of Moses. He was a tall handsome old man, dressed in well-worn working clothes, and he had a long white beard. He was machining something on a lathe, and my first reaction was to say to myself: "What have you got yourself into? Obviously this guy can't be an expert on American furnaces." The results were a perfect example of how wrong one can be with first impressions.

Mr. Lurie spoke excellent English, and, when he heard my story, explained that he would have to make some measurements before he could give an opinion. The next morning he arrived in a broken-down old car and proceeded to unload some very professional and well-used meters, which were the first signs that this man was a real pro. After connecting up to the furnace, he made some tests and then explained that he would have to make some alterations to the furnace.

Having little choice, we told him to go ahead, and a few days later he returned to install the special coil that he had made. On finishing, Mr. Lurie demonstrated that the arc was now not only very stable, but never required more than 195 amperes. From that time on, the furnace worked like a charm. Later, I learned that Mr. Lurie had studied electrical engineering as a young man in Russia, and then, being a Zionist, had come as a pioneer to Palestine.

Slowly we began to try out the investment casting process, only to find that something was radically wrong. For some reason or other, our castings were all defective. Minky and I systematically made endless experiments to isolate the cause. There were many evenings when we got together in one of our apartments and would line up dozens of defective samples on the floor to see if we find some clue of where we were going wrong. All to no avail, and there was no one to ask.

After months of agony, we suddenly realized that our furnace for heating the molds was different than those used in America. Ours was oil fired, whereas in the United States they burned gas. Both types reached the same temperature, but a gas-fired furnace starts out a room temperature and gently increases the temperature. The temperature in the oil-fired furnace, however, jumps almost immediately to several hundred degrees and this thermal shock was affecting our molds.

This was typical of the sorts of problems people faced in starting a new process in a foreign environment. Israel had only very limited supplies of gas at that time, so we had had a special oil-fired furnace built. No one in the United States used anything but gas, so our particular problem was unknown. We simply couldn't have foreseen the consequences.

It was back to Lurie. This time he was away on vacation, but his son, a graduate of the Technion, was able to take very good care of us. Since we wanted to go through the beginning of the heating cycle very slowly, he built us a special electric oven for melting the wax. Then when the molds had passed through the sensitive temperature range, we transferred them to the oil-fired furnace. From then on, we were really in the precision casting business.

Although we continued to make some special sand castings, our main business was precision casting. A small part of this business was to supply the needs of local manufacturers for all sorts of small parts. However, very little machinery was being made in those days, and this market was much too small to keep even our twelve-man plant busy. Thus we had to find our own particular market.

Israel's budding economy desperately needed tools, but these were virtually unobtainable. There was no foreign currency for import. Moreover, most tools are made of forgings and there were no facilities in the country to make forgings. After a bit of experimentation we found that our precision castings were quite suited to the need and "Dok" began producing all sorts tools such as clippers for picking fruit, wire cutters, pliers, and socket wrenches.

It was an exciting time and as things began to settle down; we thought that we had it made. In Israel, however, there are always surprises. At long last we were going to see what austerity really meant.

# 30
# Tsena

As I have described Israel's early days, only occasional hints have been dropped about austerity, for that is the way we became acquainted with *tsena*—austerity. There were few references to "austerity," as such. We certainly saw no articles on how terrible things were. Changes were made quite gradually, and by 1952 we had become used to living under very difficult conditions.

Tsena was without a doubt one of the major factors in our lives, but it cannot be divorced from all sorts of other influences; in a sense it was just a part of the package. Thus, before going into the question of austerity, the stage should be set by taking a very brief look at the news of those days.

The front pages of the papers were mainly filled with international news such as the war in Korea, the death of Stalin, and the election of President Eisenhower.

Peace talks in the Middle East still dragged on endlessly with the big powers carefully looking after their own interests. In this regard it should be noted that England was now openly rearming the Arabs and the Eisenhower-Dulles U.S. foreign policy seemed to be definitely slanted toward placating the Arab states.

Terrorism and miniwars were becoming almost daily occurrences, and it seemed that each day we read of new Israeli deaths at the hands of "marauders." The Jordanians still maintained their open season on Jews who crossed invisible lines around Jerusalem and these senseless killings also seemed to be on the increase. To punctuate this violence we began during 1953 to see endless statements by Arab leaders such as:

12 February   No Room for Both Peoples (Syrian Delegate to the Mixed Armistice Commission)

5 June        Peace with Israel Impossible (General Naguib)

Immigration had dwindled considerably after the initial rush, but was still continuing at a significant rate—over twenty-three thousand in 1952. Here, of course, was the source of the austerity problem. Israel stubbornly took in all the world's homeless and endangered Jews, without having the economy needed to provide for the exploding population.

There were also articles on the front pages discussing the grand economic strategy of the government, but virtually nowhere were the terms *austerity* or *tsena* used. By looking at these old papers one would find it hard to appreciate what was really happening.

The one place where one can begin to gain some understanding of this problem is in the inside pages of the newspapers where one saw small articles such as:

(1952)

10 September     Nutrition Experts Critical of Rations

15 September     Doctors Quit Food Council in Protest

(1953)

26 January       More Food but Less Nutrition in '52

2 March          Vegetables Too Expensive for Masses

We also learned that our main source of protein was milk and this was now being dosed with 20 percent-imported milk powder. There were tiny articles outlining what the housewife could buy with her ration coupons. On 5 May 1953 we saw the following, outlining part of the monthly allotment per person:

2 100 gram meat rations (less than half a pound per month)
Noodles cut to 300 grams
750 grams of flour
White sugar on the way
April's margerine will be completed by 12 May
12 eggs per month
150 to 200 grams of carp

On 22 June we saw that the oil promised for May would only be given out on the tenth of July. Austerity, however, was more than just what one could buy with the ration coupons.

In January 1953 a series of these small notes hidden in the middle of the papers brings to light another basic issue. On 1 January the little headline read: "Price Control Lifted from Poultry." Wonderful! This meant that one was permitted to buy chickens without points. Why? For the simple reason that the farmers were unable to obtain poultry feed, and as a result of this shortage, had to slaughter their flocks.

To add insult to injury, on the fifth of January a note appeared indicating that the free market price had been lowered dramatically due to the lack of buyers. Then on 16 January price controls were reinstated since no one could afford the chicken at the free market prices.

All sorts of learned articles appeared at the time about the whys and wherefores of the economic situation, but again on the inside pages the situation was summarized. This time in a cartoon on 8 May 1953. Eli, the cartoon's philosopher said, "I don't know much about Price Equalization or proportional budget estimates, but I do know when I'm broke."

If we now look at how people lived we must be very careful to realize that there were great differences between various segments of the population.

In July 1953 there were forty-five thousand families still living in tents. This was indeed a nightmare. In the winters many of the camps were flooded and the tents were often blown away. Things got so out of hand that the army had to be called in to put things right and to care for over eleven thousand children. For these people, having the required ration coupon was not enough. In many cases they did not have jobs and money to buy even the most basic necessities.

Even with jobs and some sort of permanent housing there were problems, for money was in very short supply. Most families had a difficult time affording the rations due them. On the other hand, there were others with means. There was a prospering black market with all the variations such as illegal abattoirs where donkeys were killed and the meat sold as beef.

One day at lunch a waiter offered me steak. When I jokingly asked if it was donkey, he seriously replied, "It's neither donkey nor camel."

Still another part of the population had families on kibbutzim or moshavim, and periodically a truck would appear with all sorts of boxes from the folks at home. In a sense the Gershonis were in this group who received help, but our folks were in the United States.

We did receive packages and payed 66 percent-duty on the contents. There was also a scheme whereby families abroad could buy "skrip," which enabled the recipients to purchase food at a local ship chandler. Such advantages certainly did make our lives a bit easier, but when I look back at how the Gershonis lived, we too had problems.

Our purchase of a pasteurizer was prophetic, for the government issued advice to housewives that all milk should be boiled. The Gershonis were in good shape insofar as eggs were concerned, due to our chicken coop. We had stocked it with about ten scrawny hens and two roosters. Proper chicken feed was not available so we fed them on table scraps and they seemed to thrive.

The neighbors had thought that their "Americans" were balmy. Who ever heard of raising chickens in the city? However, everyone soon learned. While we had been in the United States, our neighbor, Tova Ben Dov, fed the chickens for us and of course enjoyed the eggs. By the time we returned, everyone had built a coop and we awoke each morning to the crowing of roosters.

The incubator and brooder, bought at Sears, were actually used to advantage, and before long, we had about fifty eggs in the incubator. Hatching time was one of great excitement and all the neighbors' kids crowded around to watch the little chicks peck their way out of the eggs. For us city folk this was quite an education.

Israeli flats are tiny, and where to put even this small incubator was a problem. We now had three children in a tiny bedroom—Judy Gershoni was born in June 1952. Davy and Jonny slept in foldaway beds, and Judy, of course, was in a crib. We solved the location of the chickens in a very logical manner. First we put the incubator under our bed.

Then when the eggs hatched the little chicks went into the brooder, which, for want of a better place, also went under the bed. For the uninitiated, chickens in a brooder make no noise and create no unpleasant odors, besides they're cute. One could not really tell that there were fifty chickens under the bed. That is unless some one spilled the beans.

That is exactly what happened one day when we entertained some American tourists. Actually, the entertainment was not what we had planned. We were trying our best to show that Israeli life was not too far from what one found in the United States, and we were doing quite well until the De Langes arrived. At the door we muttered something about don't mention the chickens. This was all David needed.

After all of the usual pleasantries he jovially asked: "Have you seen the chickens? No? Well, come on; I'll show you." Of course everyone trooped into our bedroom and David withdrew the magic sheet metal box and then opened it to display our crop of little chicks. Lovely to see, but hardly what one expects under the bed.

To be sure, our supplemental rations did make an enormous difference in our diet; however, even with the extras, my weight dropped to one hundred fifty pounds, which was five less than it had been when

I was in college over ten years before. Another more subtle sign of limited nutrition was that the various cuts on my fingers, from work in the foundry, never seemed to heal.

We really didn't dwell on the fact that perhaps we were under-nourished, but every few months we got an interesting reminder. Tourist ships had begun to visit Israel, and every so often one would arrive with friends of the family. They were all aware of our problems so they would always invite us aboard the ship for dinner and this was indeed a treat. The interesting thing, however, occurred later. After eating a meal aboard ship, we were unable to eat for three days. We simply had no appetite after this one normal meal.

Perhaps the one experience I remember the most vividly was arriving home one evening for dinner and being greeted by Marilyn. "Hal, I know you don't like white cheese, but tonight you have a simple choice. You either eat white cheese or you don't eat. That's all I could find at the grocers."

Another anecdote that also seems to stick with me is about the time Jesse Karpas, a close friend from South Africa, burst in on us. The Karpases were certainly as well equipped as anyone with the extras from family abroad, but Jesse couldn't restrain herself.

She literally exploded. "I simply have to tell somebody about the kilo of spinach I found at my greengrocer's this morning." Apparently, as she triumphantly left the shop she met an old friend from South Africa who was in Israel on a tour. Jesse glowingly told about the kilo of spinach, only to have the woman look at her like she was out of her mind. Foreigners simply couldn't understand, and Jesse had to tell someone who would appreciate her good fortune.

Seeing to the children's diet was a worrisome task. Nothing was ever left on a plate. If one child simply could not finish, someone else ate what was left. If no one else could finish the last bit, Daddy showed the proper example. This became a household rule, and some years later it backfired.

We were on a ship going to America and as one can imagine, the meals were enormous. Each of the kids received a normal portion of which they ate perhaps a fourth. Then since nothing was to be wasted, Daddy attempted to finish what was left. Needless to say, the Israeli rule simply did not apply.

Unfortunately, austerity was not confined to food; we faced its affects in almost every conceivable way. Clothing, furniture, house-hold supplies, and electricity were all part of the picture.

Electricity was a particularly difficult commodity, for the supply was often insufficient. Hence, there were restrictions in the hours during which one could use electricity in the homes for more than simple lighting. This meant that there were days during which many house-wives could not use their stoves. It was during one of these periods that we abandoned our luxurious American electric stove for a simple kerosene cooker.

One of our first big upheavals at Dok was due to shortage of electricity, and required that we work strange shifts. For two weeks we would work from about four in the morning until noon, and with our early start-up, this was quite a hardship. Then for two weeks we would work a late shift from noon until eight at night.

An interesting variation of the shift concept was carried over to the schools. Since there were not enough buildings or teachers, some schools had two four-hour shifts, and it was even suggested that Tel Aviv go on a three-shift basis. In a similar vein, the use of vehicles was restricted to five days a week. This raised hell with running a factory outside the city, for we worked a six-day week.

Other problems were even more serious. Basic raw materials were often not available; some of our prized new plants had to close.

Phillips, which had opened a new factory for the manufacture of light bulbs, was one of our dreams come true. There had been a terrible shortage of light bulbs and Phillips stepped in to build a modern plant to solve the problem. However, when they could not get the right raw materials they decided not only to close down, but to move their plant to another country.

Similarly, another Dutch firm, the Van Leer Steel Drum Factory, shut down due to the lack of sheet steel. Still another casualty was our new automobile plant, Kaiser Fraiser, which had to lay off many of their workers due to the shortage of parts.

Most of the rest of us, however, struggled along making do with what we could scrounge locally. Many of these hardships could be borne, but then came the big problem, the general shortage of money.

When we had started thinking of the foundry there were such great shortages of everything that anything and everything could be sold. This situation lasted until just about the time that we really went into production. Then the bottom seemed to drop out of the whole market. The government in 1952 changed the exchange rates, and also imposed a capital levy on all bank accounts. Suddenly no one had any money.

This lack of money seems to have affected literally everyone, including the Gershonis. For example, one day we received a call from some tourists, who were old friends of the family, and they kindly invited us to dinner at their hotel. There was one problem, however. Marilyn's "good" dress was at the cleaners and we did not have the money to collect it. Having "nothing to wear" was not a meaningless phrase; we solved the problem by selling some photograph records to a local shop.

A similar trauma happened at the Delanges. David was then head of administration for the Shell Company and of course had a very respectable salary. The only problem was that this did not go very far. One evening we dropped over to find the Delange household in a state of complete shock. David had ripped his "good" trousers. "You don't understand," he explained. "These are the trousers I wear to work and I don't have another pair that are suitable."

Businesses had no money so they couldn't buy, and more important, couldn't pay. Perhaps the most vivid memory I have of this was at payroll time one month. We had no money to pay our men. How do you face your crew under these circumstances? Murray Greenfield managed to scrape up one hundred twenty pounds (about one hundred dollars) and we called the men together. I explained that we had not been able to collect the sums owed us, and were going to advance everyone ten pounds (about nine dollars) until we could collect the rest of their money.

Of course they understood, but Murray finished our little meeting with the advice that everyone should buy their groceries on credit and assure the grocer that they would pay up in the near future. Since that was what they had been doing anyway, it seemed to work out.

We were certainly not alone, for the entire country was facing such problems. The Tel Aviv municipality payed its temporary workers their May salaries on the tenth of July. Over one thousand teachers went on strike in Jerusalem when their pay was unduly delayed.

By today's standards it was pretty grim, but I wouldn't want to leave this subject without explaining that even under these conditions life went on. One must remember that you are viewing these days through eyes oriented to a completely different historical and social picture.

We had lived through World War II and everyone, even the Americans, were used to shortages. The most important influence, however, was the Holocaust which, to us, made building the Jewish State so very important. So despite the austerity, we attempted to live normal lives.

Our folks came to visit and became acquainted with our new baby, our friends, and our way of life. They toured the country and stayed in the little hotels of Tel Aviv that had all of twenty to thirty rooms. In essence they saw that, despite the limitations of the economic situation, we did pretty much the same things that people were doing elsewhere. Of course we griped about the latest meat ration and the shortage of laundry soap, but life went on.

Perhaps the *Times* of London of 7 January gives a neater summary of the situation. "There are startling changes in Israel; the entire population is working to lay the foundation of the future state."

However, no matter how you put it, that is the way it was.

# 31
# The Way It Is

Forty years have passed, our children are beginning to take over, and our grandchildren are growing up. We had lovely dreams, but what have we really accomplished? A few numbers may help us set the stage. The Jewish population of about 672,000 in 1949 has grown to over 3.4 million out of a total population of over 4.2 million in 1984. Our industries' exports of $16.5 million in 1949 have grown to over $5.8 billion in 1984. After 2,000 years we have rebuilt the Jewish Homeland.

One of Israel's main exports is agricultural products, so no one gets ecstatic over a kilo of spinach anymore. Our army is quite capable of protecting the country and we have a munitions industry that supplies a significant part of our needs. Perhaps even more important to the average citizen is that Israel is a country where one can feel free to walk the streets at night.

We are at peace with our most powerful neighbor, Egypt, and our borders are quiet. We have very close relations with the United States, and are optimistic about the future. However, spectacular as they may be, statistics have no flavor. To appreciate what has happened here one needs to see the country and how the people live.

A simple drive about the countryside reveals green fields, forests, towns, and lovely settlements in a land that was mostly wilderness forty years ago. The supermarkets are full and one can even buy kosher frozen pizza or Chinese egg rolls. If you would prefer, we could go to one of the shopping malls, or perhaps wander down any of our main shopping streets like Dizengoff in Tel Aviv. There you will find the stores filled with your every need.

This afternoon, how about a swim or a walk along the beach promenade in Tel Aviv? We could visit a museum or you might prefer a picnic in the park. If sports are your hobby, there's no shortage; you can even watch your game at home on television.

In the evening, what would you prefer, a symphony concert or perhaps more intimate chamber music? Would you like something lighter such as a play or a movie? Afterward we can stop at any one of many sidewalk cafés to have a cup of coffee and some pastry. If you go for nightclubs you can have your pick.

Israeli Jews are at home in their own country and when little Uri tells his momma that someone called him a dirty Jew, she gives him a bath.

To be sure, there are many less complimentary things about Israel and reveling in our *tsouris* ("troubles") seems to be a very popular exercise. Ours is a very controversial society and it is said that with two Jews you'll have three opinions.

Israel is a difficult country and we still have a long list of problems that must be solved. To go into all of these would take not just a chapter, or even a book, but a whole encyclopedia; hence, let's accept the fact that we still have a long way to go. Having said this, let me add just one observation about our difficulties.

In the course of our sabbaticals over the years, Yona and I have seen that every country has its share of problems. However, a sociological comparison of national *tsouris* would have little meaning. In every country people come to terms with their problems and attempt to deal with them. IRA terrorism, the Mafia, Irangate, Watergate, McCarthyism, you name it. These are all worrisome issues but in a healthy democracy these come to light and attempts are made to improve conditions.

Over the hundreds of years of each nation's history the solutions to such crises have each made their contribution to a better future. Unfortunately, we have only been in business for forty years; it will take a number of generations to catch up.

Perhaps the most impressive example of how the Israeli public deals with its national crises happened after the Sabra and Shatilla massacre in 1982. On 17 September someone's troops went on a rampage in the Sabra and Shatilla Palestine refugee camps, murdering hundreds of people. In the wake of this outrage there were all sorts of questions to be answered. Were Israeli troops involved? Was our high command responsible?

Prime Minister Begin was quite anxious to simply deny any responsibility in the affair and to let it die a natural death. However, rumors persisted, implying that Israelis were somehow responsible. The public's need to know what happened blossomed into a grass roots demand for a full-fledged statutory examination of this tragedy. The Israeli public insisted on knowing the facts and on calling to account the guilty parties, if they were in truth, Israelis.

Then, less than a week after we heard about Sabra and Shaltilla, it was announced, in the newspapers, that at eight'o'clock, 26 September, there would be a public demonstration in the square before the Tel Aviv municipality.

Yona and I felt that we really ought to go just to identify with the cause but we had no idea that about 10 percent of the entire population were going to join us. We live about a twenty-minute walk from the municipality, so we left in good time, and as soon as we reached our corner, we were shocked to see waves of people all going in the same direction.

Along the way every possible parking place was taken and there were all sorts of huge trucks parked on the sidewalks. Obviously, people had come from all over the country to participate. On reaching the municipality, we saw thousands and thousands of others who, like us, wanted to identify with a government of law and order.

The police estimated that four hundred thousand people took part. Since then I've been amused to read in the papers about "huge" demonstrations abroad in which twenty thousand people took part. The crowd was quiet and orderly until we heard a familiar cry. "Begin, Begin, Begin." The bullyboys, who favored the Begin and Sharon policy of a cover-up, were evidently there in force and were out to disrupt the proceedings.

At this point I was convinced that violence was about to break out all around us, but then there appeared more policemen then I had ever seen in one place. They literally seemed to spring up from the pavement. Quietly they wound their way through the crowd in the direction of the disturbance, and then the shouting stopped. A short time later the policemen seemed to be moving in the other direction. That was the last of the disturbances.

There was exactly one hour of speeches; no one spoke for more than five minutes. The speakers made it clear that the people would not allow the issue to be brushed aside and many shades of opinion were expressed. Then it was over, and we all walked home with a glorious feeling that we lived in a country where the average person could speak up and make his voice heard.

On the twenty-ninth of September a proper committee was established in law, with all the necessary powers instituted.

No, Israeli troops did not take part. It was implied, however, that some senior officials of the government and army might have done more to prevent the tragedy. As a result of these conclusions, the defense minister, Ariel Sharon, left the defense ministry, and there were changes in the command structure of the army. The important fact was that the public could demand and receive an accounting from the government on such a sensitive issue.

Perhaps the one phrase that best describes the Israeli public is that people care about our heritage. The trial of Ivan Demjanjuk, suspected of being "Ivan the Terrible" of the Treblinka concentration camp, is an excellent example.

The live radio broadcasts and evening television summaries were all widely followed by the public. Whenever I would stop at a red light, it surprised me to hear that people in the cars around me were also listening to the trial. On buses the drivers usually keep their radios tuned down so as not to disturb the riders. However, during the trial everyone could listen, and no one complained.

Whole busloads of schoolchildren were brought to sit in on the proceedings. As one youngster explained, "We've heard about the Holocaust, but it's hard for us to really understand what happened. Now, this is perhaps one of the last opportunities for us to see and hear about that period from those who survived."

A few weeks ago we celebrated the fortieth anniversary of the refugee ship *Exodus* whose passengers were so cruelly prevented from reaching Palestine by the British. On successive evenings we saw a special two-part show devoted to the event. The format was a get-together in what appeared to be a large restaurant with the guests seated around tables. The saga was relived on the screen and various guests described their particular parts in the drama.

Virtually every television set in the country was tuned in to the program, for this one had to see. In the course of the two evenings we saw how these pathetic remnants of European Jewery attempted to reach Palestine, their only hope, only to be turned back by the British. In their own way they refused all compromises, and as conditions aboard ship deteriorated to the worst imaginable, they were ultimately returned to Germany. This was the most inhuman blow that could be dealt these wretched people.

As the passengers told of their personal experiences, over and over again we heard them say, "You see, we are here." Then one of the would-be immigrants told how amid the filth and squalor, without any assistance from the British, his wife gave birth to a daughter. It was impossible to believe that the mother and child could have survived, but then he turned to a lovely-looking woman sitting beside his wife, and introduced his daughter.

However, the real shock came a moment later when it was explained that there were indeed other *Exodus* children born aboard ship. With that, these *Exodus* children were asked to come forward to the front of the hall. To everyone's amazement, around forty men and women stepped forward, and again we heard, "You see, we're here."

There couldn't have been many dry eyes in the entire country. Even today, after forty years since the *Exodus* and several weeks since the television program, I find it difficult to see the screen of my word processor, as I too remember. This is what it's all about.

Our current news sensation, and indeed the biggest story that has been in the papers for many many months, is the arrival of Ida Nudel. Her sixteen-year struggle to leave the Soviet Union has been an inspiration to not only the Russian Jews, but the Israeli public as well.

Every paper had banner headlines and featured her arrival comment, "Some hours ago I was almost a slave in Moscow. Now, I'm a free person in my own country." You would think that we are attempting to solve our water shortage, for again there were very few dry eyes in Israel.

The interesting thing about this particular incident was expressed by Shimon Peres, our foreign minister, who said at the welcoming ceremony, "A night like tonight can only happen here—not in any other country or to any other people. This is really Jewish, really Israel. It is what really makes us."

I must close now. We have talked about all sorts of good things and also recognized that there are bad things as well. However, I would like to leave you with a thought that always comes to my mind at times like these.

My father was a dress manufacturer and each season when the salesmen returned from their sales trips they would all get together to discuss how things were going. It was always the same story. "Daisy May Frocks has a much more stylish line." "You should see the fabrics that Ginsberg and Son are using this season. Their line sells itself." Then everyone would go into ecstasy over the low prices of the dresses offered by Wonder Girl. It seemed that everyone else had something easy to sell, and their own line was a real problem.

At that time my father would step in and say, "Boys, our line is like a baby. One must admit that the upstairs neighbors have a brighter child. That kid is a genius. Downstairs the new baby is a real beauty and, if we're honest, she's really prettier than our baby. Have you ever noticed the kid across the hall? He's a giant, much stronger than our baby."

"It all may be true, but remember one thing, when it's your baby you've got to love it."

That's the way it is.

## DATE DUE

| | |
|---|---|
| | |
| | |
| | |
| | |
| | |
| | |
| | |
| | |
| | |
| | |
| | |